A JOURNEY
of COURAGE

FROM DISABILITY TO
SPIRITUAL ABILITY

A Journey of Courage: From Disability to Spiritual Ability

Bahá'í Quotations © Bahá'í International Community

Compiled by Frances Mezei and Shirlee Smith

Publication © National Spiritual Assembly of the Bahá'ís of Australia Inc.
Published January 2023
All Rights Reserved

Originally published by Nine Pines Publishing, 2002

ISBN 978-1-925320-30-5

Printed with permission by
Bahá'í Distribution Services of Australia
173 Mona Vale Rd, Ingleside NSW, 2101

bds@bahai.org.au
www.bahaibooks.com.au

He that hath Me not is bereft of all things. Turn ye away from all that is on earth and seek none else but Me. I am the Sun of Wisdom and the Ocean of Knowledge. I cheer the faint and revive the dead. I am the guiding Light that illumineth the way. I am the royal Falcon on the arm of the Almighty. I unfold the drooping wings of every broken bird and start it on its flight.

Bahá'u'lláh, Tablets of Bahá'u'lláh

CONTENTS

Acknowledgements

The compilers would like to express their heartfelt appreciation, love and gratitude to the following Institutions and individuals who encouraged us with this project. Warmest appreciation to Counsellor David Smith for sharing the vision of an accessible Bahá'í Community and supporting this undertaking from the very beginning. Gratitude to the National Spiritual Assembly of the Bahá'ís of Canada for lovingly guiding us through the process of preparing this compilation and providing the literature review and approval for publication. Grateful thanks to the National Spiritual Assembly of the Bahá'ís of the United Kingdom for permission to reprint the statement "A Bahá'í Perspective on Disability". Special thanks to Auxiliary Board Member for Propagation, Meim Smith, for her inspiration and support and to the National Literature Committee for providing assistance and expertise which helped to make this compilation much more than initially envisioned.

We would also like to thank Patrick Cross for painstakingly spending many hours typing and retyping the draft manuscript; Dale Sims and Bill Sims for carefully editing the manuscript and generously offering their time to share their creative ideas, love and encouragement; and Brit Regan, who has since passed to the next world, for her moral support and belief in this undertaking.

Warmest appreciation to Beverly Davis and Linda Bishop for their loving support, encouragement, and offering valuable suggestions.

Foreword

Central to the teachings of the Bahá'í Faith is the fundamental belief that all human beings have been created to know and worship God, and to promote an ever-advancing civilization. As creations of God, we each have the capacity to do this. Yet each individual enters the world with a unique complement of faculties, attributes and capacities and, therefore, with a unique potential to fulfill his or her ultimate destiny as a servant of humankind.

The purpose of the journey of life, then, is for each individual to unleash the potential with which he or she has been endowed, regardless of the material condition. It is this complement of faculties, attributes and capacities that defines us and is the medium through which the human spirit expresses itself in service to God and humankind. The journey of life provides the opportunity to unleash the full potential inherent in each of us regardless of ability or disability.

'Abdu'l-Bahá explains that "...the honour and distinction of the individual consist in this, that he among all the world's multitudes should become a source of social good. Is any larger bounty conceivable than this, that an individual, looking within himself, should find that by the confirming grace of God he has become the cause of peace and well-being, of happiness and advantage to his fellow men?"[1]

---

1   'Abdu'l-Bahá, *The Secret of Divine Civilization*

It is this message of the Bahá'í Teachings, applicable to all, that this compilation addresses with such vividness and clarity.

The reader will find this publication a source of true enlightenment concerning the nature of disability. By drawing our attention to the power of the human spirit and how it can be triumphant, it sheds light on what it means to be human—on becoming a noble being. This compilation of quotes will also bring joy to every soul longing for meaning and understanding when faced with circumstances he or she finds both challenging and disconcerting. As explained by 'Abdu'l-Bahá: "Anybody can be happy in the state of comfort, ease, health, success, pleasure and joy; but if one will be happy and contented in the time of trouble, hardship and prevailing disease, it is the proof of nobility."[2]

Indeed, this compilation is a celebration of life, where disability becomes ability, where struggle becomes strength, and where the effort to fully participate in the building of all that is noble and good is rewarded with victory after victory. As such, it is destined to serve as a wonderful source of insight and comfort to individuals, families and health care providers alike, assisting all who read it to understand what it means to truly embrace, in unity, the diversity of humankind.

2　'Abdu'l-Bahá, *Bahá'í World Faith*, p. 363

The compilers of this publication, all of whom are intimately aware of how society perceives disability, celebrate, in their own lives, the freedom of the human spirit to express itself in service to humanity. This compilation is a signal example of their devotion to such freedom. They are to be commended for their vision in conceiving of this most valuable contribution, and for their accomplishment in assembling such a treasure of quotes.

David and Meim Smith
Toronto, Canada

Introduction

The Sacred Writings of the Bahá'í Faith provided inspiration and guidance to the compilers on how to cope with their own disabilities or afflictions and to support family members and friends who are disabled. Thus the idea was born to produce a compilation from the Writings entitled, *"A Journey of Courage: From Disability to Spiritual Ability"*, to share with others who may benefit from discovering the beauty, simplicity and pearls of wisdom found in the Divine Teachings on this theme. Our purpose is to offer an approach to transform our limitations and attitudes when dealing with our disabilities, with loved ones who are disabled or suffering from an illness, and with caregivers. This search led us to the discovery that many members of the Holy Family also suffered from disabilities and afflictions which are referred to in the compilation. It is hoped that this compilation will expand the reader's understanding and attitude toward persons with disabilities.

Coping with a disability from birth or with one acquired due to an accident, illness, or the aging process requires enormous effort and determination to function effectively with daily activities and to feel positive about ourselves. This includes deafness, blindness, mental, emotional, mobility, neurodiversity when it comes to the learning processes, and diseases of various kinds. The Universal House of Justice, in a letter dated 11 September 1995 to the National Spiritual Assembly of the Bahá'ís of the United States, stresses that "All of us suffer from imperfections which we must struggle to overcome and we all need one another's understanding and patience." Also, in the same letter they state "Whether deficiencies are inborn or acquired, our purpose in this life is to overcome them and to train ourselves in accordance with the pattern that is revealed to us in the divine Teachings." This statement provided a focus for the compilers in selecting which writings and stories to include in the compilation.

Our disabilities and struggles are given to us as gifts from God for our moral and spiritual development. Using the guidance, comfort and hope drawn from the Bahá'í Writings, we can recreate and train ourselves in new skills, attitudes and approaches to cope with our daily lives. By rising above our limitations and imperfections, the real essence of our spirit will become liberated and purified, our eyes will 'see', our ears will 'hear', our hearts will 'know' and our tongues will 'speak'. As Bahá'u'lláh states, "Then will the manifold favors and outpouring grace of the holy and everlasting Spirit confer such new life upon the seeker that he will find himself endowed with a new eye, a new ear, a new heart, and a new mind."[3]

We gain hope and inspiration when families, parents, caregivers, service and health care providers and institutions demonstrate care, love, patience and compassion in the training and support of persons with disabilities in their families and communities, undeterred by seemingly insurmountable obstacles. This quotation confirms the responsibility of the community, "...and other members who for valid reasons are incapacitated—the blind, the old, the deaf—their comfort must be looked after. In the village no one will remain in need or in want. All will live

---

3 *Gleanings from the Writings of Bahá'u'lláh*, sec. CXXV

in the utmost comfort and welfare."[4] Specific examples of service include training a child who is deaf and hard of hearing to learn communication skills, assisting a person who is permanently disabled from an accident to readjust to their new physical limitations and to grieve over the loss of a body part or function; helping a senior who is frail and has low vision to attend community functions; and living with a family member who suffers from a crippling and long-lasting degenerative disease, etc. It takes sensitivity, creativity and an openness to work out the solutions. It is often wise to consult with the person with the disability or affliction on how to deal with his or her specific situation and you will find that he or she is usually pleased to be asked.

The compilation includes 'Guidelines for Improving Accessibility', which provides practical information to guide and assist readers to improve accessibility for persons with disabilities in order to remove the barriers for their full participation in everyday community life. It outlines general guidance when planning public events as well as specific guidelines to assist persons who are deaf and hard of hearing, and have visual and mobility disabilities.

Since the book was published in 2002, there have been great developments in science, medicine, technology and resources which have transformed the lives of many to live as productive members of society. There has been advancement in our communities as we learn to apply the knowledge from the experiences and perspectives of persons with disabilities, which can take us a step further in collectively learning about diversity and inclusion in our community relationships.

---

4 'Abdu'l-Bahá, *Foundations of World Unity*

The compilers hope that reading this compilation will be as much of a joyful discovery for you as it has been for us, in seeking out the physical and spiritual truths leading *"From Disability to Spiritual Ability."* By the study and application of the teachings included in the compilation, it is our belief and hope that the lives of persons with disabilities, their families and communities will be enriched and illumined.

Frances Mezei, 2022

A Bahá'í Perspective of Disability

Written by the National Spiritual Assembly of the Bahá'ís of the United Kingdom, January, 2000

The Bahá'í approach towards social issues, such as attitudes to people with disabilities, is grounded in the belief that men and women are in essence spiritual beings located within the material creation. The material world is seen as providing the environment within which the soul can learn what it is and to what purpose it exists, and is able to develop those spiritual qualities and virtues which survive and have value beyond its life in the material realm. Bahá'í teachings draw an analogy with the embryo within its mother's womb as the embryo develops, it acquires senses, organs and limbs the utility of which only become apparent after birth.

However this analogy does not imply a correlation between the worth and condition of the soul and the physical body of the individual. Bahá'u'lláh[5] made this clear: 'Know thou that the soul of man is exalted above, and is independent of all infirmities of body or mind ... the soul itself remaineth unaffected by any bodily ailments. Consider the light of the lamp. Though an external object may interfere with its radiance, the light itself continueth to shine with undiminished power.'[6] This and many other passages in Bahá'í scripture make it quite clear

---

5   Bahá'u'lláh, Prophet Founder of the Bahá'í Faith, 1817-1892.
6   *Gleanings from the Writings of Bahá'u'lláh*

that physical disability or illness, no matter how severe, cannot in themselves bring any change in the inherent condition of the soul. As Bahá'u'lláh says: 'The spirit is permanent and steadfast in its station'. The human soul neither becomes ill from the diseases and disabilities of the body nor is cured by its health; infirmities of the body do not imply weakness, feebleness or sinfulness of spirit.[7]

From the Bahá'í perspective, recognising the essential spiritual nature of humankind in no way implies indifference to our material nature and physical well-being. Far from despising the human body and its care, Bahá'í writings describe it as 'the temple of the spirit' and place considerable emphasis on cleanliness, refinement and delicacy in matters of the person, moderation in matters of diet, and concern and care for the sick and incapacitated. Indeed, Bahá'u'lláh described the science of medicine as 'the most important of all the sciences'.[8]

A recent statement from the Bahá'í International Community put this concept into a wider context: '... Bahá'u'lláh's message is an exposition of reality as fundamentally spiritual in nature, and of the laws that govern that reality's operation. It not only sees the individual as a spiritual being, a "rational soul", but also insists that the entire enterprise that we call civilisation is itself a spiritual process, one in which the human mind and heart have created progressively more complex and efficient means to express their inherent moral and intellectual capacities.'[9]

---

7 Compilation on Health and Healing, in *Compilation of Compilations, vol. 1*, p. 478

8 Tablet to a Physician, quoted in *Bahá'u'lláh and the New Era*

9 Bahá'í International Community, *Who is Writing the Future?*, 1998

The acceleration of this process of civilisation in recent years has not only seen previously unimaginable advances in science and technology, the best fruits of which hold out breathtaking possibilities for the relief of suffering and enhancement of life, but an equally profound changing of social attitudes, including those towards the socially disadvantaged.

Throughout most of history, it has been assumed, often with the agreement of organised religion that poverty and social disadvantage of any kind were enduring and inescapable features of the social order and easing their effects was a matter for charity. Now, however, this mind-set is being widely rejected. In theory at least, government is increasingly regarded as essentially a trustee responsible to ensure the well-being of all of society's members. Germany and Great Britain introduced the first national legislation relating to social security and disability insurance, in 1884 and 1897 respectively, thus giving first effect to this changed perception, though their motives were essentially pragmatic. The scope and provisions of these first legislative steps have been extended during the ensuing century both within those countries and to most industrialised countries throughout the world. Social welfare remains a pressing subject of legislative and community concern.

The Bahá'í approach to social problems is rooted in concepts of justice, service, and the application of the principle of consultation as the means of problem resolution, all based on a belief in the essential unity of humankind. These concepts have been applied from the earliest days of the Bahá'í Faith in fields such as human rights, fostering of racial tolerance, and promoting the equality of women and men. They reflect a fundamental belief that society should be ordered in such a way that every individual, whatever his or her gender, race or physical circumstances, should have every reasonable opportunity to fully develop his or her potential, live a rewarding life, and make a positive contribution to society at large.

'Disability' as a generic term embraces a wide range of conditions. But however widely or narrowly the term is applied, being disabled implies a need for additional consideration from society beyond that normally extended to the 'able'. The Bahá'í view is that concern and care for people with disabilities and those who are ill is not a responsibility only of government as the trustee for society's well-being, but that private charity (organized and individual) should also play a role. In this way we all play our part in shouldering their social responsibilities towards others.

Application of the principle of equity that as far as possible all members of society should be treated equally and have equality of opportunity should not obscure the fact that each individual is different. For those with some form of disability, social equity requires not that the disability should be ignored, but that circumstances should not inordinately disadvantage them.

Developments in science and medicine have already transformed the lives of many who a century ago would have been condemned to depend on charity and have enabled them instead to live as full members of society. Scientific advancement is extolled in the Bahá'í writings as a noble and praiseworthy human endeavour. Developments in such fields as genetics, biochemistry and transplant surgery promise further thrilling possibilities in overcoming once intractable conditions. The Bahá'í writings broadly anticipate and encourage these developments. That the application of such developments sometimes poses ethical dilemmas reflects the lack of a commonly-held moral framework within which to judge such questions.

Many issues need to be evaluated within the wider vision provided by the Bahá'í writings on human life and its value. These writings envisage a world in which the enormous capacity of humankind: '...will be consecrated to such ends as will extend the range of human inventions and technical development, to the increase of the productivity of mankind, to the extermination of disease, to the extension of scientific research, to the raising of the standard of physical health, to the sharpening and refinement of the human brain ... to the prolongation of human life, and to the furtherance of any other agency that can stimulate the intellectual, the moral, and spiritual life of the entire human race.'[10]

As the many implications of the concept of the unity of mankind, enunciated more than a century ago by Bahá'u'lláh, take hold in the world at large, Bahá'ís believe that the obligation, both moral and utilitarian, to ensure the full integration of the disabled and disadvantaged into society will be increasingly recognised, and that the enormous resources now dissipated on war and economic conflict will be channelled into turning this obligation into reality.

~∽

---

10 Shoghi Effendi, *World Order of Bahá'u'lláh*

A JOURNEY
of COURAGE

FROM DISABILITY TO
SPIRITUAL ABILITY

PHYSICAL DISABILITY

Although the body was weak and not fitted to undergo the vicissitudes of crossing the Atlantic, yet love assisted us, and we came here. At certain times the spirit must assist the body. We cannot accomplish really great things through physical force alone; the spirit must fortify our bodily strength. For example, the body of man may be able to withstand the ordeal of imprisonment for ten or fifteen years under temperate conditions of climate and restful physical routine. During our imprisonment in Akká means of comfort were lacking, troubles and persecutions of all kinds surrounded us, yet notwithstanding such distressful conditions, we were able to endure these trials for forty years. The climate was very bad, necessities and conveniences of life were denied us, yet we endured this narrow prison forty years. What was the reason? The spirit was strengthening and resuscitating the body constantly. We lived through this long, difficult period in the utmost love and heavenly servitude. The spirit must assist the body under certain conditions which surround us, because the body of itself cannot endure the extreme strain of such hardships.

The human body is in reality very weak; there is no physical body more delicately constituted. One mosquito will distress it; the smallest quantity of poison will destroy it; if respiration ceases for a moment, it will die. What instrument could be weaker and more delicate? A blade of grass severed from the root may live an hour, whereas a human body deprived of its forces may die in one minute. But in the proportion that the human body is weak, the spirit of man is strong. It can control natural phenomena; it is a supernatural power which transcends all contingent beings. It has immortal life, which nothing can destroy or pervert. If all the kingdoms of life arise against the immortal spirit of man and seek its destruction, this immortal spirit, singly and alone, can withstand their attacks in fearless firmness and resolution because it is indestructible and empowered with supreme natural virtues ... How wonderful it is! It can attain to the Kingdom of God. It can penetrate the mysteries of the divine Kingdom and attain to everlasting life. It receives illumination from the light of God and reflects it to the whole universe. How wonderful it is! How powerful the spirit of man, while his body is so weak! If the susceptibilities of the spirit control him, there is no created being more heroic, more undaunted than man; but if physical forces dominate, you cannot find a more cowardly or fearful object because the body is so weak and incapable. Therefore, it is divinely intended that the spiritual susceptibilities of man should gain precedence and overrule his physical forces. In this way he becomes fitted to dominate the human world by his nobility and stand forth fearless and free; endowed with the attributes of eternal life.

'Abdu'l-Bahá, *The Promulgation of Universal Peace*

There is another: this body becomes weak or heavy or sick, or it finds health; it becomes tired or rested; sometimes the hand or leg is amputated, or its physical power is crippled; it becomes blind or deaf or dumb; its limbs may become paralyzed; briefly, the body may have all the imperfections. Nevertheless, the spirit in its original state, in its own spiritual perception, will be eternal and perpetual; it neither finds any imiperfection, nor will it become crippled. But when the body is wholly subjected to disease and misfortune, it is deprived of the bounty of the spirit, like a mirror which, when it becomes broken or dirty or dusty, cannot reflect the rays of the sun nor any longer show its bounties.

'Abdu'l-Bahá, Some Answered Questions

If, for example, one be endowed with the senses of hearing, of taste, of smell, of touch—but be deprived of the sense of sight, it will not be possible for one to gaze about; for sight cannot be realized through hearing or tasting, or the sense of smell or touch. In the same way, with the faculties at man's disposal it is beyond the realm of possibility for him to grasp that unseeable Reality, holy and sanctified above all the sceptics' doubts. For this, other faculties are required, other senses; should such powers become available to him, then could a human being receive some knowledge of that world; otherwise, never.

'Abdu'l-Bahá, Selections from the Writings of 'Abdu'l-Bahá

Desperate designs to poison Bahá'u'lláh and His companions, and thereby reanimate his own defunct leadership, began, approximately a year after their arrival in Adrianople, to agitate his mind. Well aware of the erudition of his half-brother, Áqáy-i-Kalím, in matters pertaining to medicine, he, under various pretexts, sought enlightenment from him regarding the effects of certain herbs and poisons, and then began, contrary to his wont, to invite Bahá'u'lláh to his home, where, one day, having smeared His tea-cup with a substance he had concocted, he succeeded in poisoning Him sufficiently to produce a serious illness which lasted no less than a month, and which was accompanied by severe pains and high fever, the aftermath of which left Bahá'u'lláh with a shaking hand till the end of His life.

Shoghi Effendi, God Passes By

As the caravan pushed forward, light snow powdered the ground, and sharp winds produced a passage of sheer torture. Frequent stops and outdoor camps were necessary whenever travel became too arduous, discomfort too acute ... The boy 'Abbás ('Abdu'l-Bahá) was inadequately clad, for there had not been time nor money to prepare for the frigid days in the saddle. He was exposed to the boreal winds for long periods of time and suffered frostbite of his feet and fingers, injuries creating chronic and recurrent pain and discomfort for his lifetime.

David S. Ruhe, Robe of Light, p. 166

'Abdu'l-Bahá invited my father and me to visit Him one evening at His home in San Francisco. When we entered His room, the Master was reclining against the pillows on His bed, and one of His secretaries was massaging His feet and ankles. The Master explained that His feet caused Him great pain, which was eased by massage. We knew that 'Abdu'l-Bahá suffered much as a result of frostbite from walking and riding in the snow during the exile of the Holy Family in Turkey, and also because of the heavy chains which He had been forced to wear part of the time on His ankles while in prison.

Ramona Allen Brown, Memories of 'Abdu'l-Bahá, p. 75

Hájí Mírzá Haydar-'Alí writes in the *Bihjatu's-Sudúr* of the hopes of the Bahá'ís that, as the heir to Bahá'u'lláh, 'Abdu'l-Bahá would, with the passage of years, come to resemble Him physically as well; but their hopes did not materialize, because sorrows and tribulations pressed hard upon 'Abdu'l-Bahá, afflictions weakened His frame and made Him a prey to a number of ailments. He goes on to say that 'Abdu'l-Bahá, in order to protect His followers from worry and anxiety, would not expose them to the knowledge of His maladies which at times were severe. However, physicians advised Him that He ought to seek a change of air, and leave the Holy Land. But subsequent events demonstrated the fact that 'Abdu'l-Bahá, when He did this, was not just embarking on a journey to improve His health in a different setting, or to prevent its further deterioration. He was indeed taking the first step to reach the world of the West and deliver, in person, the Message of His Father.

H. M. Balyuzi, 'Abdu'l-Bahá: The Centre of the Covenant of Bahá'u'lláh, p. 133

On 8 April the Greatest Holy Leaf wrote a general letter ... "Since the ascension of our Beloved 'Abdu'l-Bahá Shoghi Effendi has been moved so deeply ... that he has sought the necessary quiet in which to meditate upon the vast task ahead of him, and it is to accomplish this that he has temporarily left these regions. During his absence he has appointed me as his representative..."

It all looked very calm on paper but behind it was a raging storm in the heart and mind of Shoghi Effendi. "He has gone", the Greatest Holy Leaf wrote, "on a trip to various countries." He left with his cousin and went to Germany to consult doctors. I remember he told me they found he had almost no reflexes, which they considered very serious. In the wilderness, however, he found for himself a partial healing, as so many others had found before him. Some years later, in 1926, to Hippolyte Dreyfus, who had known him from childhood and whom he evidently felt he could be open with as an intimate friend, he wrote that his letter had reached him "on my way to the Bernese Oberland which has become my second home. In the vastnesses and recesses of its alluring mountains I shall try to forget the atrocious vexations which have afflicted me for so long ... It is a matter which I greatly deplore, that in my present state of health, I feel the least inclined to, and even incapable of, any serious discussion on these vital problems with which I am confronted and with which you are already familiar. The atmosphere in Haifa is intolerable and a radical change is impracticable. The transference of my work to any other centre is unthinkable, undesirable and in the opinion of many justly scandalous ... I cannot express myself more adequately than I have for my memory has greatly suffered."

Rúhíyyih Rabbani, The Priceless Pearl, pp. 57-58

On the evening of May 22, 1844, the Báb declared His mission to Mullá Husayn, who became the first believer in the new Dispensation, The Bábí Faith.

Mullá Husayn was very young and so frail physically that his hand shook when he wrote, but he was eager of heart and steadfast of soul, and longed with his whole being for the coming of the Promised One.

Mary Perkins, Hour of the Dawn: The Life of the Báb, p. 9

Spiritual Disability

It behoveth thee to look with divine insight upon the things We have revealed and sent unto thee and not towards the people and that which is current amongst them. They are in this day like unto a blind man who, while moving in the sunshine, demandeth: Where is the sun? Is it shining? He would deny and dispute the truth, and would not be of them that perceive. Never shall he be able to discern the sun or to understand that which hath intervened between him and it.

Bahá'u'lláh, Tablets of Bahá'u'lláh, p. 186

Say: So great is the glory of the Cause of God that even the blind can perceive it, how much more they whose sight is sharp, whose vision is pure. The blind, though unable to perceive the light of the sun, are, nevertheless, capable of experiencing its continual heat. The blind in heart, however, among the people of the Bayán—and to this God is My witness—are impotent, no matter how long the Sun may shine upon them, either to perceive the radiance of its glory, or to appreciate the warmth of its rays.

Bahá'u'lláh, Gleanings from the Writings of Bahá'u'lláh

They who reject the truth have said: 'When were the heavens cleft asunder?' Say: 'While ye lay in the graves of waywardness and error.' Among the faithless is he who rubbeth his eyes, and looketh to the right and to the left. Say: 'Blinded art thou. No refuge hast thou to flee to.' And among them is he who saith: 'Have men been gathered together?' Say: 'Yea, by My Lord! whilst thou didst lie in the cradle of idle fancies.'

Bahá'u'lláh, Writings of Bahá'u'lláh, Tablet of Ishraqát

Materialists who reason in this way, and contend that we are unable to see the world of spirit, or to perceive the blessings of God, are surely like the animals who have no understanding; having eyes they see not, ears they have, but do not hear. And this lack of sight and hearing is a proof of nothing but their own inferiority; of whom we read in the Qur'án, 'They are men who are blind and deaf to the Spirit.' They do not use that great gift of God, the power of the understanding, by which they might see with the eyes of the spirit, hear with spiritual ears and also comprehend with a Divinely enlightened heart.

'Abdu'l-Bahá, Paris Talks

Illumined by the spirit through the instrumentality of the soul, man's radiant intelligence makes him the crowning-point of Creation.

But on the other hand, when man does not open his mind and heart to the blessing of the spirit, but turns his soul towards the material side, towards the bodily part of his nature, then is he fallen from his high place and he becomes inferior to the inhabitants of the lower animal kingdom. In this case the man is in a sorry plight! For if the spiritual qualities of the soul, open to the breath of the Divine Spirit, are never used, they become atrophied, enfeebled, and at last incapable; whilst the soul's material qualities alone being exercised, they become terribly powerful...

'Abdu'l-Bahá, Paris Talks

Physical & Spiritual Barriers

Wings that are besmirched with mire can never soar.
Bahá'u'lláh, Epistle to the Son of the Wolf

Human attitudes must not be limited; for God is unlimited, and whosoever is the servant of the threshold of God must, likewise, be free from limitations.
'Abdu'l-Bahá, The Promulgation of Universal Peace

These tests, even as thou didst write, do but cleanse the spotting of self from off the mirror of the heart, till the Sun of Truth can cast its rays thereon; for there is no veil more obstructive than the self, and however tenuous that veil may be, at the least it will completely shut a person out, and deprive him of his portion of eternal grace.
'Abdu'l-Bahá, Selections from the Writings of 'Abdu'l-Bahá

The child must not be oppressed or censured because it is undeveloped; it must be patiently trained.
'Abdu'l-Bahá, The Promulgation of Universal Peace

O thou son of the Kingdom! All things are beneficial if joined with the love of God; and without His love all things are harmful and act as a veil between man and the Lord of the Kingdom.

'Abdu'l-Bahá, *Selections from the Writings of 'Abdu'l-Bahá*

Just as the earth attracts everything to the centre of gravity, and every object thrown upward into space will come down, so also material ideas and worldly thoughts attract man to the centre of self. Anger, passion, ignorance, prejudice, greed, envy, covetousness, jealousy and suspicion prevent man from ascending to the realms of holiness, imprisoning him in the claws of self and the cage of egotism. The physical man, unassisted by the divine power, trying to escape from one of these invisible enemies, will unconsciously fall into the hands of another. No sooner does he attempt to soar upward than the density of the love of self, like the power of gravity, draws him to the centre of the earth. The only power that is capable of delivering man from this captivity is the power of the breaths of the Holy Spirit.

'Abdu'l-Bahá, *Bahá'í Readings*, p. 305

O God, my God! Fill up for me the cup of detachment from all things, and in the assembly of Thy splendors and bestowals, rejoice me with the wine of loving Thee. Free me from the assaults of passion and desire, break off from me the shackles of this nether world, draw me with rapture unto Thy supernal realm, and refresh me amongst the handmaids with the breathings of Thy holiness.

'Abdu'l-Bahá, *Bahá'í Prayers*

The Glory rest upon thee, and upon whosoever turneth toward and gazeth on the Kingdom of the All-Glorious, which the Lord hath sanctified beyond the understanding of those who are neglectful of Him, and hath hid from the eyes of those who show Him pride.

'Abdu'l-Bahá, Selections from the Writings of 'Abdu'l-Bahá

If a pupil is told that his intelligence is less than his fellow pupils, it is a very great drawback and handicap to his progress. He must be encouraged to advance by the statement, "You are most capable, and if you endeavor, you will attain the highest degree."

'Abdu'l-Bahá, The Promulgation of Universal Peace

We must never dwell too much on the attitudes and feelings of our fellow-believers towards us. What is most important is to foster love and harmony and ignore any rebuffs we may receive; in this way the weaknesses of human nature and the peculiarity or attitude of any particular person is not magnified, but pales into insignificance in comparison with our joint service to the Faith we all love.

On behalf of Shoghi Effendi, Lights of Guidance, p. 116

Sarah Jane Farmer (1847-1916), a descendent of a distinguished New England family, founded Green Acre, Maine, United States, in 1894. Her vision of Green Acre as a place where various people, philosophies and religions could offer their knowledge and talents occurred in June, 1892.

Sarah suffered a serious fall in 1907 and became an invalid for the rest of her life. Fillmore Moore pressed her to surrender her right of trustee appointment. In 1908 controversy frequently erupted during meetings. Toward the end of the 1909 season, Fillmore Moore issued a bitter public statement. By 1910, as a result of both physical and psychological stress, Sarah had become gravely debilitated. Well-meaning friends, misunderstanding her condition, placed her in a private sanatorium in Portsmouth, New Hampshire.

Green Acre Bahá'í School Council, Green Acre on the Piscataqua, p. 41

The Cause of God is exalted above the world of humanity. In order to embrace it, man must acquire divine qualities. Here, self and worldly ambitions become great barriers. The test of man, therefore, is to subdue his own self. Without this he cannot recognize the Prophet. For the Manifestation of God has two natures, the divine and the human. The former is always hidden by the latter. Only those who have spiritual eyes can penetrate through the veil of human limitations and behold the reality of the Manifestation. Those who are spiritually blind are tested by the personality of the Prophet. They can see only the human qualities and often seek to find fault with these Holy Souls.

After recognition of the Manifestation, the believer will be tested by God in many ways. Each time he passes a test, he will acquire greater spiritual insight and will grow stronger in faith. The closer he gets to the person of the Manifestation the more difficult become his tests. It is then that any trace of ambition or ego may imperil his spiritual life.

Adib Taherzadeh, The Revelation of Bahá'u'lláh, vol. 1, p. 129

The possession of earthly goods is often misunderstood to be the only form of attachment. But this is not so. Man's pride in his accomplishments, his knowledge, his position, his popularity within society and, above all, his love for his own self are some of the barriers which come between him and God. To rid oneself of these attachments is not easy. It can be a painful process and may indeed prove to be a spiritual battle which lasts a lifetime.

Adib Taherzadeh, The Revelation of Bahá'u'lláh, vol. 1, p. 77

It is often attachment to this world which clouds the vision and makes the individual proud, arrogant and self-centered. Obedience to Bahá'u'lláh, humility, and submissiveness towards the Institutions will, in the end, confer inestimable blessings upon the soul.

Attachment to this world is often mistakenly understood to be the possession of earthly goods. "Should a man," Bahá'u'lláh explains to His followers, "wish to adorn himself with the ornaments of the earth, to wear its apparels, or partake of the benefits it can bestow, no harm can befall him, if he alloweth nothing whatever to intervene between him and God, for God hath ordained every good thing, whether created in the heavens or in the earth, for such of His servants as truly believe in Him."

There is a story in Persian which throws some light on the nature and meaning of detachment from this world. It is the story of a King and a dervish. The King had many spiritual qualities but in his heart he envied the dervish who seemed to have no attachment to this world. For all that a dervish possessed was a basket in which he carried his food. He spent his time roaming around town chanting the praises of his Lord and having mystical communion with Him. He had no home and no belongings yet he considered himself to be so rich that he owned the whole world. To this way of life the King was attracted, so he invited a dervish to his palace in order to learn some lessons in detachment. The dervish came and stayed for some time. At last the King decided to give up his throne and live the life of a dervish. Putting on some old clothes, he disguised himself as a poor man and left his palace with his guest.

They had walked together some distance when the dervish realized that he had left his basket behind in the palace. He explained to the King that he could not go without the basket and that they had better go back and fetch it. It was by this incident that the dervish was finally tested and found to be attached to this world. The King had left behind his palaces and his treasures and was treading the path of detachment, whereas the dervish preaching this very virtue for a life-time proved in the end to be attached to his small basket.

Attachment is an attitude of mind and is not necessarily related to riches. The pride which the individual may have in his learning and knowledge, his accomplishments in this life, his position in the community, his fame and popularity, the love of his own self and of his possessions could all become barriers between his soul and God.

Adib Taherzadeh, Trustees of the Merciful, pp. 46-48

TESTS & DIFFICULTIES

The more difficulties one sees in the world the more perfect one becomes. The more you plough and dig the ground the more fertile it becomes. The more you cut the branches of a tree the higher and stronger it grows. The more you put the gold in the fire the purer it becomes. The more you sharpen the steel by grinding the better it cuts. Therefore, the more sorrows one sees the more perfect one becomes. That is why, in all times, the Prophets of God have had tribulations and difficulties to withstand. The more often the captain of a ship is in the tempest and difficult sailing the greater his knowledge becomes. Therefore I am happy that you have had great tribulations and difficulties. For this I am very happy - that you have had many sorrows. Strange it is that I love you and still I am happy that you have sorrows.

'Abdu'l-Bahá, Star of the West, vol. 14, p. 41

To sum it up, the Ancient Beauty was ever, during His sojourn in this transitory world, either a captive bound with chains, or living under a sword, or subjected to extreme suffering and torment, or held in the Most Great Prison. Because of His physical weakness, brought on by His afflictions, His blessed body was worn away to a breath; it was light as a cobweb from long grieving. And His reason for shouldering this heavy load and enduring all this anguish, which was even as an ocean that hurleth its waves to high heaven - His reason for putting on the heavy iron chains and for becoming the very embodiment of utter resignation and meekness, was to lead every soul on earth to concord, to fellow-feeling, to oneness; to make known amongst all peoples the sign of the singleness of God, so that at last the primal oneness deposited at the heart of all created things would bear its destined fruit, and the splendour of 'No difference canst thou see in the creation of the God of Mercy,' would cast abroad its rays.

'Abdu'l-Bahá, *Selections from the Writings of 'Abdu'l-Bahá*

Anybody can be happy in the state of comfort, ease, health, success, pleasure and joy; but if one will be happy and contented in the time of trouble, hardship and prevailing disease, it is the proof of nobility.

'Abdu'l-Bahá, *Bahá'í World Faith, p. 363*

Affliction beat upon this captive like the heavy rains of spring, and the victories of the malevolent swept down in a relentless flood, and still 'Abdu'l-Bahá remained happy and serene, and relied on the grace of the All-Merciful. That pain, that anguish, was a paradise of all delights, those chains were the necklace of a king on a throne in heaven. Content with God's will, utterly resigned, my heart surrendered to whatever fate had in store, I was happy. For a boon companion, I had great joy.

Finally a time came when the friends turned inconsolable, and abandoned all hope. It was then the morning dawned, and flooded all with unending light. The towering clouds were scattered, the dismal shadows fled. In that instant the fetters fell away, the chains were lifted off the neck of this homeless one and hung round the neck of the foe. Those dire straits were changed to ease, and on the horizon of God's bounties the sun of hope rose up. All this was out of God's grace and His bestowals.

And yet, from one point of view, this wanderer was saddened and despondent. For what pain, in the time to come, could I seek comfort? At the news of what granted wish could I rejoice? There was no more tyranny, no more affliction, no tragical events, no tribulations. My only joy in this swiftly-passing world was to tread the stony path of God and to endure hard tests and all material griefs. For otherwise, this earthly life would prove barren and vain, and better would be death. The tree of being would produce no fruit; the sown field of this existence would yield no harvest. Thus it is my hope that once again some circumstance will make my cup of anguish to brim over, and that beauteous Love, that Slayer of souls, will dazzle the beholders again. Then will this heart be blissful, this soul be blessed.

'Abdu'l-Bahá, Selections from the Writings of 'Abdu'l-Bahá

The Guardian urges you not to be discouraged by any setbacks you may have. Life is a process of trials and testings, and these are—contrary to what we are prone to thinking—good for us, and give us stamina, and teach us to rely on God. Knowing He will help us, we can help ourselves more.

Shoghi Effendi, Unfolding Destiny, p. 453

We should not, however, forget that an essential characteristic of this world is hardship and tribulation and that it is by overcoming them that we achieve our moral and spiritual development. As the Master says, sorrow is like furrows, the deeper they go, the more plentiful is the fruit we obtain.

Shoghi Effendi, The Bahá'í Life, p. 3

O thou who art firm in the Covenant! ... Praise thou God that in tests thou art firm and steadfast and art holding fast to the Abhá Kingdom. Thou art not shaken by any affliction or disturbed by any calamity. Not until man is tried doth the pure gold distinctly separate from the dross. Torment is the fire of test wherein the pure gold shineth resplendently and the impurity is burned and blackened. At present thou art, praise be to God, firm and steadfast in tests and trials and art not shaken by them.

'Abdu'l-Bahá, Selections from the Writings of 'Abdu'l-Bahá

...as we suffer these misfortunes we must remember that the Prophets of God Themselves were not immune from these things which men suffer. They knew sorrow, illness and pain too. They rose above these things through Their spirits, and that is what we must try and do too, when afflicted. The troubles of this world pass, and what we have left is what we have made of our souls; so it is to this we must look—to becoming more spiritual, drawing nearer to God, no matter what our human minds and bodies go through.

Shoghi Effendi, The Bahá'í Life, p. 16

The road is stony, and there are many tests; but as you say, if the friends will learn to live according to Bahá'u'lláh's teachings, they will discover that they work indeed in mysterious and forceful ways; and that there is always help at hand, that obstacles are overcome, and that success is assured in the end.

On behalf of Shoghi Effendi, Living the Life, p. 36

Naturally there will be periods of distress and difficulty, and even severe tests; but if that person turns firmly towards the divine Manifestation, studies carefully His spiritual teachings and receives the blessings of the Holy Spirit, he will find that in reality these tests and difficulties have been the gifts of God to enable him to grow and develop.

On behalf of Shoghi Effendi, Living the Life, pp. 35-36

History has shown that many eminent men have achieved greatness merely by facing hardships and difficulties. Through perseverance and steadfastness they have overcome obstacles, demonstrated their strength of character and revealed the hidden powers latent within them. In contrast, the weak and feeble have often succumbed to such difficulties and perished. Clearly, suffering reveals the strength, the character and the faith of every human being. The greater the cause, the more strenuous are the tests and trials to which the individual is subjected. In this Dispensation, from amidst the blood-baths of martyrdom, great heroes have emerged whose lives have illumined the history of the Cause of God by their courage and self-sacrifice.

Adib Taherzadeh, The Revelation of Bahá'u'lláh, vol. 1, p. 270

Ethel's (Rosenberg) poor health—particularly concerning her chest and her eyes—was now indeed causing her extreme distress. She was forced to cancel her meetings for teaching the Cause and at one stage was even taken into hospital for an operation. The Holy Family were most concerned and in several letters assured her of their thoughts and prayers. Ethel had hoped to accompany Laura Barney on a trip to Persia but her physical condition would not allow it. Munavvar (a daughter of 'Abdu'l-Bahá) particularly sympathized with Ethel's frustration and expressed how hard it was to "be so caged up as we are and be prevented from doing which you like best to do and the most interested in (sic). But perhaps it has to be so for some wisdom which we do not know. Of course how can the limited mind of man know the mysteries of the great wisdom of God."

Robert Weinberg, Ethel Jenner Rosenberg: The Life and Times of England's Outstanding Bahá'í Pioneer Worker, pp. 81-82

Dorothy Baker, Hand of the Cause, prepared this talk, "The Spiritual Life of Man," for a radio program in Lima, Ohio, United States.

One day a businessman said to me, 'Secretly I wonder about myself. I arise in the morning, eat, keep shop, sleep and then do it all over again. I begin to feel like that person who said, "Man matters only to himself; he is fighting a lone fight against a vast indifference."'

What a strange creature man is! He stands at the very apex of creation and forgets his own preciousness in the sight of God. Sometimes we go into dark closets of our own building and stuff up the keyhole and the cracks. Then we say, 'The sun is not shining for me.' We build the closets of our own odd variety of materials - envy, fear, selfishness, sadness and sometimes just a sense of frustration and futility. And there we stay, mainly because we have not thought out our position there and so we are not doing anything about it. Often we hear the sighs of others in nearby closets and we wish we could liberate them, but not having freed ourselves, we find it pretty hard to tell them what to do.

Now the first thing that is probably needed is a larger perspective. I had the good fortune to have a remarkable grandmother. How well I remember hearing her say, 'If anything troubles you very much now, look at it in terms of five years from this time, or twenty-five, or fifty, and if it still looms pretty large, measure it in terms of eternity. Now that is my theme this morning - measure your life and everything in it in terms of eternity. Then look back, if you will, and wonder what became of your darkest closet.

The great thing is to find for ourselves the purpose of being, and to hold to that thru everything. Bahá'u'lláh said, 'O God, I testify that thou hast created me to know Thee and to adore Thee.' There is God at the far end and here are we at the near end, on this lonely little island, the earth, needing to discover in that brief flash, an enormous purpose like that! And it is brief! He also said, 'Count all the days of thy life as less than a fleeting instant.'

To know and adore God! Think of the things we deplore every day that all the while may be really speeding us on our way! Take the matter of trouble, for example. Bahá'u'lláh, in His tablet to the Sháh of Persia, wrote, 'I am not impatient of calamity in His way nor of affliction for His love. God hath made afflictions as a morning shower to His green pasture, and as a wick for His lamp, whereby earth and Heaven are illumined.'

A morning shower! Often trouble opens the heart to God. And after that it becomes purified, little by little, so that the self or Satan of the heart dies out and makes room for the Divine Beloved. I came just this morning upon these words, 'Purify thy heart for My descent. The Friend and stranger cannot dwell there together.' Trouble is often just the testing ground of the soul. There is a real freedom in it. As a Kreisler after difficult years of drudgery is free in the world of music, as an athlete after long discipline of the body has supremacy in the world of sports, so does your soul win a sovereignty thru a life that challenges it to be at grips with the world. Tests often come again and again to teach a single lesson, until at last there is a victory and a former weakness is replaced by strength. Every time this happens, it marks a milestone on the path to God.

Dorothy Freeman, From Copper to Gold: The Life of Dorothy Baker, pp. 149-150

Responsibilities of the Community

Therefore strive that your actions day by day may be beautiful prayers. Turn towards God, and seek always to do that which is right and noble. Enrich the poor, raise the fallen, comfort the sorrowful, bring healing to the sick, reassure the fearful, rescue the oppressed, bring hope to the hopeless, shelter the destitute!

This is the work of a true Bahá'í, and this is what is expected of him. If we strive to do all this, then are we true Bahá'ís, but if we neglect it, we are not followers of the Light, and we have no right to the name.

God, who sees all hearts, knows how far our lives are the fulfillment of our words.

'Abdu'l-Bahá, Paris Talks

O ye lovers of this wronged one! Cleanse ye your eyes, so that ye behold no man as different from yourselves. See ye no strangers; rather see all men as friends, for love and unity come hard when ye fix your gaze on otherness.

'Abdu'l-Bahá, Selections from the Writings of 'Abdu'l-Bahá

Wherefore must the friends of God, with utter sanctity, with one accord, rise up in the spirit, in unity with one another, to such a degree that they will become even as one being and one soul. On such a plane as this, physical bodies play no part, rather doth the spirit take over and rule; and when its power encompasseth all then is spiritual union achieved. Strive ye by day and night to cultivate your unity to the fullest degree.

'Abdu'l-Bahá, Selections from the Writings of 'Abdu'l-Bahá

Concern yourselves with one another. Help along one another's projects and plans. Grieve over one another. Let none in the whole country go in need. Befriend one another until ye become as a single body, one and all...

'Abdu'l-Bahá, Consultation (compilation)

Then the orphans will be looked after, all of whose expenses will be taken care of. The cripples in the village—all their expenses will be looked after. The poor in the village—their necessary expenses will be defrayed. And other members who for valid reasons are incapacitated—the blind, the old, the deaf—their comfort must be looked after. In the village no one will remain in need or in want. All will live in the utmost comfort and welfare. Yet no schism will assail the general order of the body politic.

'Abdu'l-Bahá, Foundations of World Unity

...close your eyes to the deficiencies of other souls.

'Abdu'l-Bahá, Selections from the Writings of 'Abdu'l-Bahá

Be ye loving fathers to the orphan, and a refuge to the helpless, and a treasury for the poor, and a cure for the ailing. Be ye the helpers of every victim of oppression, the patrons of the disadvantaged. Think ye at all times of rendering some service to every member of the human race. Pay ye no heed to aversion and rejection, to disdain, hostility, injustice: act ye in the opposite way. Be ye sincerely kind, not in appearance only. Let each one of God's loved ones centre his attention on this: to be the Lord's mercy to man; to be the Lord's grace. Let him do some good to every person whose path he crosseth, and be of some benefit to him. Let him improve the character of each and all, and reorient the minds of men. In this way, the light of divine guidance will shine forth, and the blessings of God will cradle all mankind: for love is light, no matter in what abode it dwelleth; and hate is darkness, no matter where it may make its nest. O friends of God! That the hidden Mystery may stand revealed, and the secret essence of all things may be disclosed, strive ye to banish that darkness for ever and ever.

'Abdu'l-Bahá, *Selections from the Writings of 'Abdu'l-Bahá*

We must associate with all humanity in gentleness and kindliness. We must love all with love of the heart. Some are ignorant; they must be trained and educated. One is sick; he must be healed. Another is as a child; we must assist him to attain maturity. We must not detest him who is ailing, neither shun him, scorn nor curse him, but care for him with the utmost kindness and tenderness.

'Abdu'l-Bahá, *The Promulgation of Universal Peace*

To look after the sick is one of the greatest duties! Every soul who becomes sick, the other friends should certainly offer the life (of service) in the utmost kindness.

We should all visit the sick. When they are in sorrow and suffering it is a real help and benefit to have a friend come. Happiness is a great healer to those who are ill. In the east it is the custom to call upon the patient often and meet him individually. The people in the east show the utmost kindness and compassion to the sick and suffering. This has greater effect than the remedy itself. You must always have this thought of love and affection when you visit the ailing and afflicted.

'Abdu'l-Bahá, The Pattern of Bahá'í Life (compilation)

Wherefore must the loved ones of God associate in affectionate fellowship with stranger and friend alike, showing forth to all the utmost loving-kindness, disregarding the degree of their capacity, never asking whether they deserve to be loved. In every instance let the friends be considerate and infinitely kind. Let them never be defeated by the malice of the people, by their aggression and their hate, no matter how intense. If others hurl their darts against you, offer them milk and honey in return; if they poison your lives, sweeten their souls; if they injure you, teach them how to be comforted; if they inflict a wound upon you, be a balm to their sores; if they sting you, hold to their lips a refreshing cup.

'Abdu'l-Bahá, Selections from the Writings of 'Abdu'l-Bahá

Praised be God, the women believers have organized meetings where they will learn how to teach the Faith, will spread the sweet savours of the Teachings and make plans for training the children ... Let them also study whatever will nurture the health of the body and its physical soundness, and how to guard their children from disease.

'Abdu'l-Bahá, *Selections from the Writings of 'Abdu'l-Bahá*

You must consider all His servants as your own family and relations. Direct your whole effort toward the happiness of those who are despondent, bestow food upon the hungry, clothe the needy, and glorify the humble. Be a helper to every helpless one, and manifest kindness to your fellow creatures in order that ye may attain the good pleasure of God. This is conducive to the illumination of the world of humanity and eternal felicity for yourselves.

'Abdu'l-Bahá, *The Promulgation of Universal Peace*

The second attribute of perfection is justice and impartiality ... It means to consider the welfare of the community as one's own. It means, in brief, to regard humanity as a single individual, and one's own self as a member of that corporal form, and to know of a certainty that if pain or injury afflicts any members of that body, it must inevitably result in suffering for all the rest.

'Abdu'l-Bahá, *The Secret of Divine Civilization*

O ye lovers of God! Be kind to all peoples; care for every person; do all ye can to purify the hearts and minds of men; strive ye to gladden every soul. To every meadow be a shower of grace, to every tree the water of life; be as sweet musk to the sense of humankind, and to the ailing be a fresh, restoring breeze. Be pleasing waters to all those who thirst, a careful guide to all who have lost their way; be father and mother to the orphans; be loving sons and daughters to the old; be an abundant treasure to the poor. Think ye of love and good fellowship as the delights of heaven; think ye of hostility and hatred as the torments of hell.

'Abdu'l-Bahá, *Selections from the Writings of 'Abdu'l-Bahá*

The future of Mount Carmel is very bright. I can see it now covered all over with a blanket of light. I can see many ships anchored at the Port of Haifa. I can see the kings of the earth with vases of flowers in their hands walking solemnly toward the Shrine of Bahá'u'lláh and the Báb with absolute devotion and in a state of prayer and supplication. At the time that they put a crown of thorns on His head, Christ could see the kings of the earth bowing before Him, but others could not see this.

And now I can see not only powerful lamps which will floodlight this mountain brightly, but I can also see Houses of Worship, hospitals, schools, homes for the handicapped, orphanages and all the other humanitarian institutions erected on Mount Carmel.

'Abdu'l-Bahá, *quoted by Adib Taherzadeh, The Covenant of Bahá'u'lláh, p. 226*

The interests of the blind, too, have not been neglected by that alert and enterprising community, as is shown by the placing of Bahá'í books, transcribed by its members in Braille, in thirty libraries and institutes, in eighteen states of the United States of America, in Honolulu (Hawaii), in Regina (Saskatchewan), and in the Tokyo and Geneva Libraries for the Blind, as well as in a large number of circulating libraries connected with public libraries in various large cities of the North American continent.

Shoghi Effendi, God Passes By

When a Bahá'í finds it essential to seek the help of others, and after his own efforts and those of his family and close friends have proved inadequate, he may certainly turn to his Local Spiritual Assembly, which will consult on his problem, extend a helping hand to him, if the conditions of the Local Fund permit, and even more importantly, will counsel and advise him on what opportunities are open to him, and what steps he might take to seek a solution to his problem. If the Local Assembly feels that the help or guidance of the National Assembly should be sought, it will no doubt refer the matter to the National Assembly.

On behalf of the Universal House of Justice, Lights of Guidance, p. 123

By the Sacred Verse: 'Begging is forbidden, and it is also prohibited to dispense alms to a beggar' is meant that mendicancy is forbidden and that giving charity to people who take up begging as their profession is also prohibited. The object is to wipe out mendicancy altogether. However, if a person is disabled, stricken by dire poverty or becomes helpless, then it is incumbent upon the rich or the trustees to provide him with a monthly allowance for his subsistence. When the House of Justice comes into being it will set up homes for the incapacitated. Thus no one will be obliged to beg, even as the supplementary part of the Blessed Verse denotes: 'It is enjoined upon everyone to earn his livelihood'; then He says: As to those who are disabled, it devolveth upon the trustees and the rich to make adequate provision for them.' By 'trustees' is meant the representatives of the people, that is to say the members of the House of Justice.

On behalf of the Universal House of Justice, Lights of Guidance, p. 120

Marjory Morten, an early Bahá'í, wrote about The Greatest Holy Leaf Bahíyyih Khánum, sister of 'Abdu'l-Bahá and daughter of Bahá'u'lláh.

You were sure that if one tried to hurt her she would wish to console him for his own cruelty. For her love was unconditioned, could penetrate disguise and see hunger behind the mask of fury, and she knew that the most brutal self is secretly hoping to find gentleness in another.

Marjory Morten, The Passing of Bahíyyih Khánum, The Bahá'í World: 1932-34

We would ... emphasize the ideal of rehabilitation in the family as well as in the community. Family members should be trained, where possible, to help provide the support and encouragement that the disabled person requires to surmount his impairment.

Statement by the Bahá'í International Community, dated August 1988, "Human Rights and Disability" to the United Nations

UNITY IN DIVERSITY

The Blessed Beauty saith: 'Ye are all the fruits of one tree, the leaves of one branch.' Thus hach He likened this world of being to a single tree, and all its peoples to the leaves thereof, and the blossoms and fruits. It is needful for the bough to blossom, and leaf and fruit to flourish, and upon the interconnection of all parts of the world-tree, dependeth the flourishing of leaf and blossom, and the sweetness of the fruit.

'Abdu'l-Bahá, Selections from the Writings of 'Abdu'l-Bahá

Consider the flowers of a garden: Though differing in kind, color, form and shape, yet, inasmuch as they are refreshed by the waters of one spring, revived by the breath of one wind, invigorated by the rays of one sun, this diversity increaseth their charm, and addeth unto their beauty ... How unpleasing to the eye if all the flowers and plants, the leaves and blossoms, the fruits, the branches and the trees of that garden were all of the same shape and color! Diversity of hues, form and shape, enricheth and adorneth the garden, and heighteneth the effect thereof. In like manner, when divers shades of thought, temperament and character are brought together under the power and influence of one central agency, the beauty and glory of human perfection will be revealed and made manifest. Naught but the celestial potency of the Word of God, which ruleth and transcendeth the realities of all things, is capable of harmonizing the divergent thoughts, sentiments, ideas, and convictions of the children of men.

'Abdu'l-Bahá, Selections from the Writings of 'Abdu'l-Bahá

When a person becomes a Bahá'í, he gives up the past only in the sense that he is a part of this new and living Faith of God, and must seek to pattern himself, in act and thought, along the lines laid down by Bahá'u'lláh. The fact that he is by origin a Jew or a Christian, a black man or a white man, is not important any more, but, as you say, lends color and charm to the Bahá'í community in that it demonstrates unity in diversity.

On behalf of Shoghi Effendi, Bahá'í News, no. 251, January 1952

FAITH

The first sign of faith is love.
'Abdu'l-Bahá, The Promulgation of Universal Peace

Be confident in the bounty of thy Lord.
'Abdu'l-Bahá, Tablets of 'Abdu'l-Bahá

Faith is the magnet which draws the confirmation of the Merciful One. Service is the magnet which attracteth the heavenly strength. I hope thou wilt attain both.
'Abdu'l-Bahá, Tablets of 'Abdu'l-Bahá

The essential purpose of Faith and Belief is to ennoble the inner being of man with the outpourings of grace from on high. If this be not attained, it is indeed deprivation itself. It is the torment of infernal fire.
'Abdu'l-Bahá, The Bahá'í World: 1925-1926, p. 12

The invisible hosts of the Kingdom are ready to extend to you all the assistance you need, and through them you will no doubt succeed in removing every obstacle in your way, and in fulfilling this most cherished desire of your heart. Bahá'u'lláh has given us promise that should we persevere in our efforts and repose all our confidence in Him the doors of success will be widely open before us.

On behalf of Shoghi Effendi, The Power of Divine Assistance, pp. 49-50

Never lose thy trust in God. Be thou ever hopeful, for the bounties of God never cease to flow upon man. If viewed from one perspective they seem to decrease, but from another they are full and complete. Man is under all conditions immersed in a sea of God's blessings. Therefore, be thou not hopeless under any circumstances, but rather be firm in thy hope.

'Abdu'l-Bahá, Selections from the Writings of 'Abdu'l-Bahá

I say unto you that anyone who will rise up in the Cause of God at this time shall be filled with the spirit of God, and that He will send His hosts from heaven to help you, and that nothing shall be impossible to you if you have faith. And now I give you a commandment which shall be for a covenant between you and Me—that ye have faith; that your faith be steadfast as a rock that no storms can move, that nothing can disturb, and that it endure through all things even to the end; even should ye hear that your Lord has been crucified, be not shaken in your faith; for I am with you always, whether living or dead, I am with you to the end. As ye have faith so shall your powers and blessings be. This is the balance—this is the balance—this is the balance.

'Abdu'l-Bahá, An Early Pilgrimage, p. 40

Bahá'u'lláh and the Master have both urged us repeatedly to disregard our own handicaps and lay our whole reliance upon God. He will come to our help if we only arise and become an active channel for God's grace.

On behalf of Shoghi Effendi, The Power of Divine Assistance, pp. 47-48

Life afflicts us with very severe trials sometimes, but we must always remember that when we accept patiently the Will of God, He compensates us in other ways. With faith and love we must be patient, and He will surely reward us.

On behalf of Shoghi Effendi, Lights of Guidance, p. 603

Although you seem to feel that your prayers have not so far been answered ... the Guardian (Shoghi Effendi) wishes you nevertheless not to allow such disappointments to undermine your faith in the power of prayer, but rather to continue entreating the Almighty to enable you to discover the great wisdom which may be hidden behind all these sufferings. For are not our sufferings often blessings in disguise, through which God wishes to test the sincerity and depth of our faith, and thereby make us firmer in His Cause?

On behalf of Shoghi Effendi, Spiritual Foundations: Prayer, Meditation and the Devotional Attitude, p. 16

...when the determination is strong and the faith firm, the friends can work wonders and surprise even themselves.

On behalf of Shoghi Effendi, Unfolding Destiny, p. 156

Prayer, Meditation & Fasting

The most acceptable prayer is the one offered with the utmost spirituality and radiance; its prolongation hath not been and is not beloved by God. The more detached and the purer the prayer, the more acceptable is it in the presence of God.

The Báb, Selections from the Writings of the Báb

The wisdom of prayer is this: that it causeth a connection between the servant and the True One, because in that state man with all heart and soul turneth his face towards His Highness the Almighty, seeking His association and desiring His love and compassion.

'Abdu'l-Bahá, Tablets of 'Abdu'l-Bahá

It behooveth the servant to pray to and seek assistance from God, and to supplicate and implore His aid. Such becometh the rank of servitude, and the Lord will decree whatsoever He desireth, in accordance with His consummate wisdom.

'Abdu'l-Bahá, Spiritual Foundations: Prayer, Meditation and the Devotional Attitude, p. 9

Supplication and prayer on behalf of others will surely be effective.
'Abdu'l-Bahá, Star of the West, vol. 8, p. 47

There are two ways of healing sickness, material means and spiritual means. The first is by the treatment of physicians; the second consisteth in prayers offered by the spiritual ones to God and in turning to Him. Both means should be used and practised.
'Abdu'l-Bahá, Selections from the Writings of 'Abdu'l-Bahá

The prayers which were revealed to ask for healing apply both to physical and spiritual healing. Recite them, then, to heal both the soul and the body. If healing is right for the patient, it will certainly be granted; but for some ailing persons, healing would only be the cause of other ills, and therefore wisdom doth not permit an affirmative answer to the prayer.
'Abdu'l-Bahá, Selections from the Writings of 'Abdu'l-Bahá

Meditation is the key for opening the doors of mysteries. In that state man abstracts himself: in that state man withdraws himself from all outside objects; in that subjective mood he is immersed in the ocean of spiritual life and can unfold the secrets of things-in-themselves. To illustrate this, think of man as endowed with two kinds of sight; when the power of insight is being used the outward power of vision does not see.
'Abdu'l-Bahá, Paris Talks

...prayer and fasting is the cause of awakening and mindfulness and conducive to protection and preservation from tests.

'Abdu'l-Bahá, Tablets of 'Abdu'l-Bahá

As regards fasting, it constitutes, together with the obligatory prayers, the two pillars that sustain the revealed Law of God. They act as stimulants to the soul, strengthen, revive, and purify it, and thus insure its steady development.

Shoghi Effendi, Principles of Bahá'í Administration, p. 8

Prayer and meditation are very important factors in deepening the spiritual life of the individual, but with them must go also action and example, as these are the tangible result of the former. Both are essential.

On behalf of Shoghi Effendi, Lights of Guidance, p. 456

Such hindrances (i.e., illness and other difficulties), no matter how severe and insuperable they may at first seem, can and should be effectively overcome through the combined and sustained power of prayer and of determined and continued effort. For have not Bahá'u'lláh and 'Abdu'l-Bahá both repeatedly assured us that the Divine and unseen hosts of victory will ever reinforce and strengthen those who valiantly and confidently labour in their name? This assurance should indeed enable you to overcome any feeling of unworthiness, of incapacity to serve, and any inner or outer limitation which threatens to handicap your labours for the Cause. You should therefore arise, and with a heart filled with joy and confidence endeavour to contribute any share that is in your power toward the wider diffusion and greater consolidation of our beloved Faith.

On behalf of Shoghi Effendi, Living the Life, p. 15

...unfortunately, not everyone achieves easily and rapidly the victory over self. What every believer, new or old, should realize is that the Cause has the spiritual power to re-create us if we make the effort to let that power influence us, and the greatest help in this respect is prayer. We must supplicate Bahá'u'lláh to assist us to overcome the failings in our own characters, and also exert our own will power in mastering ourselves.

On behalf of Shoghi Effendi, Lights of Guidance, p. 115

Courage

Strive as much as ye can to turn wholly toward the Kingdom, that ye may acquire innate courage and ideal power.

'Abdu'l-Bahá, *Selections from the Writings of 'Abdu'l-Bahá*

Remember not your own limitations; the help of God will come to you. Forget yourself. God's help will surely come! When you call on the Mercy of God waiting to reinforce you, your strength will be tenfold. Look at me: I am so feeble, yet I have had the strength given me to come amongst you: a poor servant of God, who has been enabled to give you this message!

'Abdu'l-Bahá, *Paris Talks*

It was Ella Bailey whom Shoghi Effendi named "the first American martyr to be laid to rest in African soil." Ella had been a cripple since childhood, never in good health, rarely free of pain. Despite her afflictions she taught the Bahá'í Faith throughout her life and made many little-known sacrifices. Ella was a living example of courage to her many friends, always happy and ready to do all she could for the Cause.

Ramona Allen Brown, *Memories of 'Abdu'l-Bahá, pp. 29-30*

In 1909, Ella Bailey received this Tablet from 'Abdu'l-Bahá.

To Ella M. Bailey,
Upon her be Bahá-Al-Abhá!
He is God!
O thou maidservant of God!

Be thou not sad on account of past vicissitudes and troubles, neither be thou discouraged by hardships and difficulties. Be thou hopeful in the Bounty of the True One, and be thou happy and rejoiced in the love of God. This world is the arena of tests, trials, and calamities. All the existing things are targets for the arrows of mortalities; therefore, one must not feel sad or disheartened on account of the travails or become hopeless over the intensity of misfortune and distress. Praise be to God that thou hast found the guidance of God, hast entered into the Kingdom of God, hast attained to peace and tranquillity, and hast obtained a share from the Everlasting Bounty and Mercy. Therefore, pass the remaining days of thy life with the utmost joy and fragrance; and, with a joyful heart and tranquil mind, live and act under the protection of His Highness, the Clement.

Upon thee be Bahá-Al-Abhá!

'Abdu'l-Bahá ABBAS.

Quoted by Ramona Allen Brown, Memories of 'Abdu'l-Bahá, p. 29

On 11 August 1911 the Master ('Abdu'l-Bahá) stepped on board the S.S. Corsica bound for Marseilles in France. 'He arose', Shoghi Effendi would recall a full century after his grandfather's birth, 'with sublime courage, confidence and resolution to consecrate what little strength remained to Him, in the evening of His life, to a service of such heroic proportions that no parallel to it is to be found in the annals of the first Bahá'í century...'

Robert Weinberg, Ethel Jenner Rosenberg: The Life and Times of England's Outstanding Bahá'í Pioneer Worker, pp. 127-128

At age thirty-five, Catherine Heward Huxtable died from the deadly effects of muscular dystrophy. Attended by her husband, Clifford "Cliff" Huxtable (1932–), Catherine passed away in 1967 at home on the remote island of St. Helena in the South Atlantic, the third and last pioneering post the Huxtables shared as a couple. Their story deserves special mention in the annals of the Ten Year Plan/World Crusade (1953–1963), not only because the Huxtables pioneered to distant lands, but more importantly because Catherine served the Bahá'í Faith while living with the challenges imposed by a physical disability that confined her to a wheelchair. With each passing year, she grew weaker, but the gradual ebbing of Catherine's powers could not dampen her determination to pioneer.

Jack McLean, A Love That Could Not Wait, preface p. vii

Accepting affliction with courage and grace, seizing the opportunities that life presents, and living life to the fullest, regardless of the length of our years, are surely the outstanding lessons of Catherine's life. The story of the wheelchair pioneer who, with the assistance of her helpmate, defied her disability confirms that her oft-repeated prayer to make her life count in the Faith she loved so well was not said in vain.

Jack McLean, A Love That Could Not Wait, preface p. ix

PHYSICAL & SPIRITUAL HEALING

Trusting in God and Determined Effort

If anyone revile you, or trouble touch you, in the path of God, be patient, and put your trust in Him Who heareth, Who seeth.

Bahá'u'lláh, Epistle to the Son of the Wolf

Rely upon God. Trust in Him. Praise Him, and call Him continually to mind. He verily turneth trouble into ease, and sorrow into solace, and toil into utter peace. He verily hath dominion over all things.

'Abdu'l-Bahá, Selections from the Writings of 'Abdu'l-Bahá

One must never consider one's own feebleness, it is the strength of the Holy Spirit of Love, which gives the power to teach. The thought of our own weakness could only bring despair.

'Abdu'l-Bahá, Paris Talks

Look not at thy weakness and impotence; nay, look at the power of thy Lord, which hath surrounded all regions.

'Abdu'l-Bahá, Tablets of 'Abdu'l-Bahá

These and other words of comfort, of strength, and of healing were spoken to a man, whose cloud of misery seemed to melt away in the warmth of the Master's ('Abdu'l-Bahá) loving presence.

Do not be filled with grief when humiliation overtaketh thee. The bounty and power of God is without limit for each and every soul in the world. Seek for spiritual joy and knowledge, then, though thou walk upon this earth, thou wilt be dwelling within the divine realm.

'Abdu'l-Bahá, quoted by Lady Blomfield, The Chosen Highway, p. 160

The greater your handicaps the firmer your determination should wax, and the more abundant will assuredly be the blessings and confirmations of Bahá'u'lláh.

Shoghi Effendi, Dawn of a New Day, p. 87

Consult a Competent Physician

Resort ye, in times of sickness, to competent physicians; We have not set aside the use of material means, rather have We confirmed it through this Pen, which God hath made to be the Dawning-place of His shining and glorious Cause.

Bahá'u'lláh, The Kitáb-i-Aqdás: The Most Holy Book

It is incumbent upon everyone to seek medical treatment and to follow the doctor's instructions, for this is in compliance with the divine ordinance, but, in reality, He Who giveth healing is God.

'Abdu'l-Bahá, Selections from the Writings of 'Abdu'l-Bahá

The secretaries of the Guardian have conveyed his guidance on this point in many letters to individual believers in passages such as these: "...refer to competent physicians and abide by their considered decisions", "... invariably consult and follow the treatment of competent and conscientious physicians...". Thus the obligation to consult physicians and to distinguish between doctors who are well trained in medical sciences and those who are not is clear, but the Faith should not be associated with any particular school of medical theory or practice. It is left to each believer to decide for himself which doctors he should consult, bearing in mind the principles enunciated above.

On behalf of the Universal House of Justice, Health and Healing (compilation)

Physical and Spiritual Healing

The powers of the sympathetic nerve are neither entirely physical nor spiritual, but are between the two. The nerve is connected with both. Its phenomena shall be perfect when its spiritual and physical relation are normal. When the material world and the divine world are well correlated, when the heart becomes heavenly and the aspirations become pure and divine, perfect connection shall take place. Then shall this power produce a perfect manifestation. Physical and spiritual diseases will then receive absolute healing.

'Abdu'l-Bahá, Tablets of 'Abdu'l-Bahá

There are two ways of healing sickness, material means and spiritual means. The first is by the treatment of physicians; the second consisteth in prayers offered by the spiritual ones to God and in turning to Him. Both means should be used and practised.

Illnesses which occur by reason of physical causes should be treated by doctors with medical remedies; those which are due to spiritual causes disappear through spiritual means. Thus an illness caused by affliction, fear, nervous impressions, will be healed more effectively by spiritual rather than by physical treatment. Hence, both kinds of treatment should be followed; they are not contradictory. Therefore thou shouldst also accept physical remedies inasmuch as these too have come from the mercy and favour of God, Who hath revealed and made manifest medical science so that His servants may profit from this kind of treatment also. Thou shouldst give equal attention to spiritual treatments, for they produce marvellous effects.

Now, if thou wishest to know the true remedy which will heal man from all sickness and will give him the health of the divine kingdom, know that it is the precepts and teachings of God. Focus thine attention upon them.

'Abdu'l-Bahá, Selections from the Writings of 'Abdu'l-Bahá

O thou distinguished physician! ... Praise be to God that thou hast two powers: one to undertake physical healing and the other spiritual healing. Matters related to man's spirit have a great effect on his bodily condition. For instance, thou shouldst impart gladness to thy patient, give him comfort and joy, and bring him to ecstasy and exultation. How often hath it occurred that this hath caused early recovery. Therefore, treat thou the sick with both powers. Spiritual feelings have a surprising effect on healing nervous ailments.

'Abdu'l-Bahá, *Selections from the Writings of 'Abdu'l-Bahá*

All true healing comes from God! There are two causes for sickness, one is material, the other spiritual. If the sickness is of the body, a material remedy is needed, if of the soul, a spiritual remedy.

If the heavenly benediction be upon us while we are being healed then only can we be made whole, for medicine is but the outward and visible means through which we obtain the heavenly healing. Unless the spirit be healed, the cure of the body is worth nothing. All is in the hands of God, and without Him there can be no health in us!

'Abdu'l-Bahá, *Paris Talks*

Disease is of two kinds: material and spiritual. Take for instance, a cut hand; if you pray for the cut to be healed and do not stop its bleeding, you will not do much good; a material remedy is needed.

Sometimes if the nervous system is paralysed through fear, a spiritual remedy is necessary. Madness, incurable otherwise, can be cured through prayer. It often happens that sorrow makes one ill, this can be cured by spiritual means.

'Abdu'l-Bahá, 'Abdu'l-Bahá in London, p. 65

All of these ailments will pass away and you will receive perfect physical and spiritual health ... Let your heart be confident and assured that through the Bounty of Bahá'u'lláh, everything will become pleasant for you ... But you must turn your face wholly towards the Abhá (All- Glorious) Kingdom, giving perfect attention—the same attention that Mary Magdalene gave to His Holiness Christ—and I assure you that you will get physical and spiritual health. You are worthy. I give you the glad tidings that you are worthy because your heart is pure ... Be confident! Be happy! Be rejoiced! Be hopeful!

'Abdu'l-Bahá, quoted by J.E. Esslemont, Bahá'u'lláh and the New Era

Know thou that every soul is fashioned after the nature of God, each being pure and holy at his birth. Afterwards, however, the individuals will vary according to what they acquire of virtues or vices in this world. Although all existent beings are in their very nature created in ranks or degrees, for capacities are various, nevertheless every individual is born holy and pure, and only thereafter may he become defiled.

And further, although the degrees of being are various, yet all are good. Observe the human body, its limbs, its members, the eye, the ear, the organs of smell, of taste, the hands, the fingernails. Notwithstanding the differences among all these parts, each one within the limitations of its own being participateth in a coherent whole. If one of them faileth it must be healed, and should no remedy avail, that part must be removed.

'Abdu'l-Bahá, Selections from the Writings of 'Abdu'l-Bahá

Thou hast written about thy poor sight. According to the explicit divine text the sick must refer to the doctor. This decree is decisive and everyone is bound to observe it. While thou art there thou shouldst consult the most skilled and the most famed eye specialist.

'Abdu'l-Bahá, Health and Healing (compilation)

With regard to your question concerning spiritual healing. Such a healing constitutes, indeed, one of the most effective methods of relieving a person from either his mental or physical pains and sufferings. 'Abdu'l-Bahá has in His 'Paris Talks' emphasized its importance by stating that it should be used as an essential means for effecting a complete physical cure. Spiritual healing, however, is not and cannot be a substitute for material healing, but it is a most valuable adjunct to it. Both are, indeed, essential and complementary.

On behalf of Shoghi Effendi, Lights of Guidance, p. 276

Just as there are laws governing our physical lives, requiring that we must supply our bodies with certain foods, maintain them within a certain range of temperatures, and so forth, if we wish to avoid physical disabilities, so also there are laws governing our spiritual lives.

Universal House of Justice, Living the Life, p. 40

The Importance of Rest and Relaxation

...you should not neglect your health, but consider it the means which enables you to serve. It—the body—is like a horse which carries the personality and spirit, and as such should be well cared for so it can do its work! You should certainly safeguard your nerves, and force yourself to take time, and not only for prayer and meditation, but for real rest and relaxation.

On behalf of Shoghi Effendi, Health and Healing (compilation)

We must not only be patient with others, infinitely patient!, but also with our own poor selves, remembering that even the Prophets of God sometimes got tired and cried out in despair! ... He urges you to persevere and add up your accomplishments, rather than to dwell on the dark side of things. Everyone's life has both a dark and bright side. The Master said: turn your back to the darkness and your face to Me.

Shoghi Effendi, Unfolding Destiny, pp. 456-457

Yet who can doubt that all the central Figures demonstrated to the whole of mankind an assured and happy way of life? Here is where their example seems particularly precious. To rise above the disappointments, obstacles, and pain which we experience in serving the Cause is difficult enough, but to be called on, in doing so, to be happy and confident is perhaps the keenest spiritual test any of us can meet. The lives of the Founders of our Faith clearly show that to be fundamentally assured does not mean that we live without anxieties, nor does being happy mean that there are not periods of deep grief when, like the Guardian, we wrap ourselves in a blanket, pray and supplicate, and give ourselves time for healing in preparation for the next great effort.

National Spiritual Assembly of Canada, quoted in Quickeners of Mankind, p. 117

Short Healing Prayer

Thy name is my healing, O my God, and remembrance of Thee is my remedy. Nearness to Thee is my hope, and love for Thee is my companion. Thy mercy to me is my healing and my succor in both this world and the world to come. Thou, verily, art the All-Bountiful, the All-Knowing, the All-Wise.

Bahá'u'lláh, Bahá'í Prayers

Happiness is a Great Healer

You must be happy always. You must be counted among the people of joy and happiness and must be adorned with divine morals. In large measure happiness keeps our health while depression of spirit begets diseases. The substance of eternal happiness is spirituality and divine morality, which has no sorrow to follow it.

'Abdu'l-Bahá, quoted in 239 Days: 'Abdu'l-Bahá's Journey in America, p. 94

Stanwood Cobb, the renowned educator wrote, "This philosophy of joy was the keynote of all 'Abdu'l-Bahá's teachings. "Are you happy?" was His frequent greeting to his visitors. "Be Happy!"

"Those who were unhappy (and who of us are not at times!) would weep at this. And 'Abdu'l-Bahá would smile as if to say, "Yes, weep on. Beyond the tears is sunshine."

"And sometimes He would wipe away with His own hands the tears from their wet cheeks, and they would leave His presence transfigured." In California it was observed that `despite the Master's fatigue at times, and His physical ailments, He welcomed everyone with a beaming smile, and in His pleasing and vibrant voice would ask, "Are you happy?" He loved the sound of laughter and often told stories and anecdotes to make us laugh. When we heard Him laugh, we knew that he or someone else had told an amusing story, and the sound of His laughter made us all happy. Once the Master told us that during the most dangerous and trying times of

His imprisonment Bahá'u'lláh would ask each member of the family to relate the most amusing incident or story they had experienced or heard that day. After the tale had been told, they would all roar with laughter.

Annamarie Honnold, Vignettes from the Life of 'Abdu'l-Bahá, p. 127 and Ramona Brown, Memories of 'Abdu'l-Bahá, p. 38

Overcoming Fear and Attaining a Peace of Mind

When thou wishest to treat nervous pains turn thy whole being to the realm on high with thine heart detached from aught else besides Him and thy soul enraptured by the love of God. Then seek confirmation of the Holy Spirit from the Abhá Kingdom, while touching the affected part with utmost love, tenderness and attraction to God. When all these things are combined, be assured that healing will take place.

'Abdu'l-Bahá, Health and Healing (compilation)

Peace of mind is gained by the centering of the spiritual consciousness on the Prophet of God; therefore you should study the spiritual Teachings, receive the Water of Life from the Holy Utterances. Then by translating these high ideals into action, your entire character will be changed, and your mind will not only find peace, but your entire being will find joy and enthusiasm.

On behalf of Shoghi Effendi, Lights of Guidance, p. 112

He will certainly pray that you may entirely overcome your fear-complex. When you concentrate your thoughts on realizing that you now belong to Bahá'u'lláh, are His servant whom He loves and will always help, if you ask Him to, and that the great spiritual strength of the Cause of God is behind you for you to draw upon, you will soon see your fears melting away.

On behalf of Shoghi Effendi, High Endeavors, p. 237

Restoring Our Faculties and Strength

O Thou kind Lord! Praise be unto Thee that Thou hast shown us the highway of guidance, opened the doors of the kingdom and manifested Thyself through the Sun of Reality. To the blind Thou hast given sight; to the deaf Thou hast granted hearing; Thou hast resuscitated the dead; Thou hast enriched the poor; Thou hast shown the way to those who have gone astray; Thou hast led those with parched lips to the fountain of guidance; Thou hast suffered the thirsty fish to reach the ocean of reality; and Thou hast invited the wandering birds to the rose garden of grace.

O Thou Almighty! We are Thy servants and Thy poor ones; we are remote and yearn for Thy presence, are athirst for the water of Thy fountain, are ill, longing for Thy healing. We are walking in Thy path and have no aim or hope save the diffusion of Thy fragrance, so that the souls may raise the cry of "O God, guide us to the straight path." May their eyes be opened to behold the light, and may they be freed from the darkness of ignorance. May they gather around the lamp of Thy guidance. May every portionless one receive a share. May the deprived become the confidants of Thy mysteries.

O Almighty! Look upon us with the glance of mercifulness. Grant us heavenly confirmation. Bestow upon us the breath of the Holy Spirit, so that we may be assisted in Thy service and, like unto brilliant stars, shine in these regions with the light of Thy guidance.

Verily, Thou art the Powerful, the Mighty, the Wise and the Seeing.

'Abdu'l-Bahá, Bahá'í Prayers

O God! O God! This is a broken-winged bird and his flight is very slow—assist him so that he may fly toward the apex of prosperity and salvation, wing his way with the utmost joy and happiness throughout the illimitable space, raise his melody in Thy Supreme Name in all the regions, exhilarate the ears with this call, and brighten the eyes by beholding the signs of guidance.

O Lord! I am single, alone and lowly. For me there is no support save Thee, no helper except Thee and no sustainer beside Thee. Confirm me in Thy service, assist me with the cohorts of Thy angels, make me victorious in the promotion of Thy Word and suffer me to speak out Thy wisdom amongst Thy creatures. Verily, Thou art the helper of the weak and the defender of the little ones, and verily Thou art the Powerful, the Mighty and the Unconstrained.

'Abdu'l-Bahá, Bahá'í Prayers

It is my hope that the breaths of the Holy Spirit will so be breathed into your hearts that your tongues will disclose the mysteries, and set forth and expound the inner meanings of the Holy Books; that the friends will become physicians, and will, through the potent medicine of the heavenly Teachings, heal the long-standing diseases that afflict the body of this world; that they will make the blind to see, the deaf to hear, the dead to come alive; that they will awaken those who are sound asleep.

'Abdu'l-Bahá, Selections from the Writings of 'Abdu'l-Bahá

He (the Guardian) does not feel you should permit your speech impediment to give you a sense of inferiority. Moses stammered! And what you are and what you believe as a Bahá'í give you a tremendous advantage over others. This does not mean that you should not make every effort to overcome it, and go to doctors for advice and assistance. He also assures you he will pray that you overcome this difficulty entirely, also that wherever you are the way will open for you to teach and serve the Faith.

On behalf of Shoghi Effendi, Unfolding Destiny, p. 446

O Ye lovers of God! The world is even as a human being who is diseased and impotent, whose eyes can see no longer, whose ears have gone deaf, all of whose powers are corroded and used up. Wherefore must the friends of God be competent physicians who, following the holy teachings, will nurse this patient back to health. Perhaps, God willing, the world will mend, and become permanently whole, and its exhausted faculties will be restored, and its person will take on such vigor, freshness and verdancy that it will shine out with comeliness and grace.

'Abdu'l-Bahá, Selections from the Writings of 'Abdu'l-Bahá

Illnesses Do Not Effect the Spirit

Let your spirit unfold the white wings of progress. Often physical sickness draws man nearer unto his Maker, suffers his heart to be made empty of all worldly desires until it becomes tender and sympathetic toward all sufferers and compassionate to all creatures. Although physical diseases cause man to suffer temporarily, yet they do not touch his spirit. Nay, rather, they contribute toward the divine purpose; that is, spiritual susceptibilities will be created in his heart.

'Abdu'l-Bahá, from Diary of Mirza Sohrab, Star of the West, vol. 8, p. 231

Concerning Mental Illness

Mental illness is not spiritual, although its effects may indeed hinder and be a burden in one's striving toward spiritual progress. In a letter written on behalf of the Guardian to a believer there is this further passage: 'Such hindrances (i.e. illness and outer difficulties), no matter how severe and insuperable they may at first seem, can and should be effectively overcome through the combined and sustained power of prayer and of determined and continued effort.'

That effort can include the counsel of wise and experienced physicians including psychiatrists. Working for the Faith, serving others who may need you, and giving of yourself can aid you in your struggle to overcome your sufferings. One helpful activity is, of course, striving to teach the Cause in spite of personal feelings of shortcomings, thus allowing the healing words of the Cause to flood your mind with their grace and positive power.

On behalf of the Universal House of Justice, Lights of Guidance, p. 284

It is not easy to be burdened with long years of mental illness such as you describe. And plainly you have sought aid from many persons of scientific and non-scientific training backgrounds, apparently to little avail over the years of your prolonged illness. Possibly you should consider, if it is feasible, consulting the best specialists in a medical centre in one of the major cities, where the most advanced diagnosis and treatment can be obtained. The science of the mind, of normality and of the disabilities from which it may suffer, is in its relative infancy, but much may be possible to aid you to minimize your suffering and make possible an active life. The last ten years in the therapy of mental disorders has seen important advances from which you may well benefit.

Your discovery of the Faith, of its healing Writings and its great purposes for the individual and for all mankind, have indeed brought to you a powerful force toward a healthy life which will sustain you on a higher level, whatever your ailment may be. The best results for the healing process are to combine the spiritual with the physical, for it should be possible for you to overcome your illness through the combined and sustained power of prayer and of determined effort.

On behalf of the Universal House of Justice, Lights of Guidance, pp. 283-284

Medical Science is Progressing

It is, therefore, evident that it is possible to cure by foods, aliments and fruits; but as today the science of medicine is imperfect, this fact is not yet fully grasped. When the science of medicine reaches perfection, treatment will be given by foods, aliments, fragrant fruits and vegetables, and by various waters, hot and cold in temperature.

This discourse is brief; but, if God wills, at another time, when the occasion is suitable, this question will be more fully explained.

'Abdu'l-Bahá, Some Answered Questions

Every day medical science is progressing, and it is quite possible that some new form of treatment or some new doctor may be able to get you on your feet. He will certainly pray that this may be so.

On behalf of Shoghi Effendi, Health and Healing (compilation)

At whatever time highly-skilled physicians shall have developed the healing of illnesses by means of foods, and shall make provision for simple foods, and shall prohibit humankind from living as slaves to their lustful appetites, it is certain that the incidence of chronic and diversified illnesses will abate, and the general health of all mankind will be much improved. This is destined to come about. In the same way, in the character, the conduct and the manners of men, universal modifications will be made.

'Abdu'l-Bahá, Selections from the Writings of 'Abdu'l-Bahá

Transformation to Physical & Spiritual Ability

At that hour will the Mystic Herald, bearing the joyful tidings of the Spirit, shine forth from the City of God resplendent as the morn, and, through the trumpet-blast of knowledge, will awaken the heart, the soul, and the spirit from the slumber of heedlessness. Then will the manifold favors and outpouring grace of the holy and everlasting Spirit confer such new life upon the seeker that he will find himself endowed with a new eye, a new ear, a new heart, and a new mind.

Bahá'u'lláh, Gleanings from the Writings of Bahá'u'lláh

The station of absolute self-surrender transcendeth, and will ever remain exalted above, every other station.

Bahá'u'lláh, Gleanings from the Writings of Bahá'u'lláh

From amongst all mankind hath He chosen you, and your eyes have been opened to the light of guidance and your ears attuned to the music of the Company above;

and blessed by abounding grace, your hearts and souls have been born into new life. Thank ye and praise ye God that the hand of infinite bestowals hath set upon your heads this gem-studded crown, this crown whose lustrous jewels will forever flash and sparkle down all the reaches of time.

'Abdu'l-Bahá, Selections from the Writings of 'Abdu'l-Bahá

The rewards of this life are the virtues and perfections which adorn the reality of man. For example, he was dark and becomes luminous; he was ignorant and becomes wise; he was neglectful and becomes vigilant; he was asleep and becomes awakened; he was dead and becomes living; he was blind and becomes a seer; he was deaf and becomes a hearer; he was earthly and becomes heavenly; he was material and becomes spiritual. Through these rewards he gains spiritual birth and becomes a new creature.

'Abdu'l-Bahá, Some Answered Questions

O thou possessor of a seeing heart! Although, materially speaking, thou art deprived of physical sight, yet, praise be to God, spiritual insight is thine. Thy heart seeth and thy spirit heareth. Bodily sight is subject to a thousand maladies and assuredly will ultimately be lost. Thus no importance should be attached to it. But the sight of the heart is illumined. It discerneth and discovereth the divine Kingdom. It is everlasting and eternal. Praise God, therefore, that the sight of thy heart is illumined, and the hearing of thy mind responsive.

'Abdu'l-Bahá, Selections from the Writings of 'Abdu'l-Bahá

The outward miracles have no importance for the people of Reality. If a blind man receive sight, for example, he will finally again become sightless, for he will die and be deprived of all his senses and powers. Therefore, causing the blind man to see is comparatively of little importance, for this faculty of sight will at last disappear. If the body of a dead person be resuscitated, of what use is it since the body will die again? But it is important to give perception and eternal life—that is, the spiritual and divine life. For this physical life is not immortal, and its existence is equivalent to nonexistence. So it is that Christ said to one of His disciples: 'Let the dead bury their dead'; for 'That which is born of the flesh is flesh; and that which is born of the Spirit is spirit.'

Observe: those who in appearance were physically alive, Christ considered dead; for life is the eternal life, and existence is the real existence. Wherever in the Holy Books they speak of raising the dead, the meaning is that the dead were blessed by eternal life; where it is said that the blind received sight, the signification is that he obtained the true perception; where it is said a deaf man received hearing, the meaning is that he acquired spiritual and heavenly hearing. This is ascertained from the text of the Gospel where Christ said: 'These are like those of whom Isaiah said, They have eyes and see not, they have ears and hear not; and I healed them.'

'Abdu'l-Bahá, *Some Answered Questions*

Reflect that light is the expression of the vibrations of the etheric matter: the nerves of the eye are affected by these vibrations, and sight is produced.

'Abdu'l-Bahá, *Some Answered Questions*

There is no doubt that it is the spirit and that there is no change or transformation in it, for it is not a composition of elements, and anything that is not composed of elements is eternal. Change and transformation are peculiarities of composition. There is no change and transformation in the spirit. In proof of this, the body may become weakened in its members. It may be dismembered, or one of its members may be incapacitated. The whole body may be paralyzed; and yet the mind, the spirit, remains ever the same. The mind decides; the thought is perfect; and yet the hand is withered, the feet have become useless, the spinal column is paralyzed, and there is no muscular movement at all, but the spirit is in the same status. Dismember a healthy man; the spirit is not dismembered. Amputate his feet; his spirit is there. He may become lame; the spirit is not affected. The spirit is ever the same; no change or transformation can you perceive, and because there is no change or transformation, it is everlasting and permanent.

Consider man while in the state of sleep; it is evident that all his parts and members are at a standstill, are functionless. His eye does not see, his ear does not hear, his feet and hands are motionless; but, nevertheless, he does see in the world of dreams, he does hear, he speaks, he walks, he may even fly in an airplane. Therefore, it becomes evident that though the body be dead, yet the spirit is alive and permanent. Nay, the perceptions may be keener when man's body is asleep, the flight may be higher, the hearing may be more acute; all the functions are there, and yet the body is at a standstill. Hence, it is proof that there is a spirit in the man, and in this spirit there is no distinction as to whether the body be asleep or absolutely dead and dependent. The spirit is not incapacitated by these conditions; it is not bereft of its existence; it is not bereft of its perfections. The proofs are many, innumerable.

'Abdu'l-Bahá, *The Promulgation of Universal Peace*

The body of man becomes lean or fat; it is afflicted with disease, suffers mutilation; perhaps the eyes become blind, the ears deaf; but none of these imperfections and failings afflict or affect the spirit. The spirit of man remains in the same condition, unchanged. A man is blinded, but his spirit continues the same. He loses his hearing, his hand is cut off, his foot amputated; but his spirit remains the same. He becomes lethargic, he is afflicted with apoplexy; but there is no difference, change or alteration in his spirit. This is proof that death is only destruction of the body, while the spirit remains immortal, eternal.

'Abdu'l-Bahá, *The Promulgation of Universal Peace*

How often do we see a man, poor, sick, miserably clad, and with no means of support, yet spiritually strong. Whatever his body has to suffer, his spirit is free and well! Again, how often do we see a rich man, physically strong and healthy, but with a soul sick unto death. It is quite apparent to the seeing mind that a man's spirit is something very different from his physical body. The spirit is changeless, indestructible. The progress and development of the soul, the joy and sorrow of the soul, are independent of the physical body.

'Abdu'l-Bahá, *Paris Talks*

O thou who art enamoured of the Covenant! The Blessed Beauty hath promised this servant that souls would be raised up who would be the very embodiments of guidance, and banners of the Concourse on high, torches of God's oneness, and stars of His pure truth, shining in the heavens where God reigneth alone. They would give sight to the blind, and would make the deaf to hear; they would raise the dead to life. They would confront all the peoples of the earth, pleading their Cause with proofs of the Lord of the seven spheres.

'Abdu'l-Bahá, Selections from the Writings of 'Abdu'l-Bahá

The confirmations of the Spirit are all those powers and gifts which some are born with and which men sometimes call genius, but for which others have to strive with infinite pains. They come to that man or woman who accepts his life with radiant acquiescence.

'Abdu'l-Bahá, 'Abdu'l-Bahá in London

Why then are ye quenched, why silent, why leaden and dull? Ye must shine forth like the lightning, and raise up a clamouring like unto the great sea. Like a candle must ye shed your light, and even as the soft breezes of God must ye blow across the world. Even as sweet breaths from heavenly bowers, as musk-laden winds from the gardens of the Lord, must ye perfume the air for the people of knowledge, and even as the splendours shed by the true Sun, must ye illumine the hearts of humankind. For ye are the life-laden winds, ye are the jessamine-scents from the gardens of the saved. Bring then life to the dead, and awaken those who slumber. In the darkness of the world be ye radiant flames; in the sands of perdition, be ye well-springs of the water of life, be ye guidance from the Lord God. Now is the time to serve, now is the time to be on fire. Know ye the value of this chance, this favourable juncture that is limitless grace, ere it slip from your hands.

'Abdu'l-Bahá, Selections from the Writings of 'Abdu'l-Bahá

[Man] must forget his own selfish conditions that he may thus arise to the station of sacrifice. It should be to such a degree that if he sleep, it should not be for pleasure, but to rest the body in order to do better, to speak better, to explain more beautifully, to serve the servants of God and to prove the truths. When he remains awake, he should seek to be attentive, serve the Cause of God and sacrifice his own stations for those of God. When he attains to this station, the confirmations of the Holy Spirit will surely reach him, and man with this power can withstand all who inhabit the earth.

'Abdu'l-Bahá, Bahá'í World Faith

...your eyes have been opened to the light of guidance and your ears attuned to the music of the Company above; and blessed by abounding grace, your hearts and souls have been born into new life.

'Abdu'l-Bahá, Selections from the Writings of 'Abdu'l-Bahá

But I mean this limitless universe is like the human body, all the members of which are connected and linked with one another with the greatest strength. How much the organs, the members and the parts of the body of man are intermingled and connected for mutual aid and help, and how much they influence one another! In the same way, the parts of this infinite universe have their members and elements connected with one another, and influence one another spiritually and materially.

For example the eye sees, and all the body is affected; the ear hears, and all the members of the body are moved. Of this there is no doubt; and the universe is like a living person. Moreover, the connection which exists between the members of beings must necessarily have an effect and impression, whether it be material or spiritual.

For those who deny spiritual influence upon material things we mention this brief example: wonderful sounds and tones, melodies and charming voices, are accidents which affect the air—for sound is the term for vibrations of the air—and by these vibrations the nerves of the tympanum of the ear are affected, and hearing results.

'Abdu'l-Bahá, Some Answered Questions

The field larks are become the festival's musicians, and lifting wondrous voices they cry and sing to the melodies of the Company on high.

'Abdu'l-Bahá, Selections from the Writings of 'Abdu'l-Bahá

Only the perceiving eye beholdeth the rays of the sun, only the listening ear can hear the singing of the Concourse on high.

'Abdu'l-Bahá, Selections from the Writings of 'Abdu'l-Bahá

Bahá'u'lláh teaches in the Mathnaví that man will not be able to receive the light of God in this day unless he acquires a new eye. Eyes which are fixed on the things of this world can never see the glory of His Revelation, and ears which are tuned to the voices of the ungodly cannot hear the melodies of the Kingdom. By 'new eyes' and 'new ears' He means spiritual eyes and spiritual ears. He states that since the eye of the spirit receives its light from God it is shameful to let it turn to a stranger, and reaffirms that the purpose of God in creating the inner eye was that man might behold the beauty of His Manifestation in this world. In *The Hidden Words* Bahá'u'lláh reveals:

O Son of Dust! Blind thine eyes, that thou mayest behold My beauty; stop thine ears, that thou mayest hearken unto the sweet melody of My voice; empty thyself of all learning, that thou mayest partake of My knowledge; and sanctify thyself from riches, that thou mayest obtain a lasting share from the ocean of My eternal wealth. Blind thine eyes, that is, to all save My beauty; stop thine ears to all save My word; empty thyself of all learning save the knowledge of Me; that with a clear vision, a pure heart and an attentive ear thou mayest enter the court of My holiness.

Adib Taherzadeh, The Revelation of Bahá'u'lláh, vol. 2, p. 31

Equal Standard of Human Rights

The standard inculcated by Bahá'u'lláh seeks, under no circumstances, to deny anyone the legitimate right and privilege to derive the fullest advantage and benefit from the manifold joys, beauties, and pleasures with which the world has been so plentifully enriched by an All-Loving Creator.

Shoghi Effendi, The Advent of Divine Justice

Bahá'u'lláh taught that an equal standard of human rights must be recognized and adopted. In the estimation of God all men are equal; there is no distinction or preferment for any soul in the dominion of His justice and equity.

'Abdu'l-Bahá, The Promulgation of Universal Peace

...there shall be an equality of rights and prerogatives for all mankind.

'Abdu'l-Bahá, The Promulgation of Universal Peace

...you are challenged and do have the obligation to uphold and vindicate the distinction between the license that limits your possibilities for genuine progress and the moderation that ensures the enjoyment of true liberty.

The Universal House of Justice, Individual Rights and Freedoms in the World Order of Bahá'u'lláh

Responsibilities

With reference to Bahá'u'lláh's command concerning the engagement of the believers in some sort of profession; the Teachings are most emphatic on this matter, particularly the statement in the "Aqdas" to this effect which makes it quite clear that idle people who lack the desire to work can have no place in the new World Order. As a corollary of this principle, Bahá'u'lláh further states that mendicity should not only be discouraged but entirely wiped out from the face of society. It is the duty of those who are in charge of the organization of society to give every individual the opportunity of acquiring the necessary talent in some kind of profession, and also the means of utilizing such a talent, both for its own sake and for the sake of earning the means of his livelihood. Every individual, no matter how handicapped and limited he may be, is under the obligation of engaging in some work or profession, for work, specially when performed in the spirit of service, is according to Bahá'u'lláh a form of worship. It has not only a utilitarian purpose, but has a value in itself, because it draws us nearer to God, and enables us to better grasp His purpose for us in this world. It is obvious, therefore, that the inheritance of wealth cannot make anyone immune from daily work.

On behalf of Shoghi Effendi, Lights of Guidance, p. 623

Examples of Individuals

Marjory Morten, an early Bahá'í, wrote about The Greatest Holy Leaf, Bahíyyih Khánum, sister of 'Abdu'l-Bahá and daughter of Bahá'u'lláh.

She did not resist the shocks and upheavals of life and she did not run counter to obstacles. She was never impatient. She was as incapable of impatience as she was of revolt. But this was not so much long-sufferance as it was quiet awareness of the forces that operate in the hours of waiting and inactivity.

Marjory Morten, The Passing of Bahíyyih Khánum, The Bahá'í World: 1932-34

Mullá Muhammad writing about Mullá Husayn.

"...I have known him from his childhood, and have been associated with him, as a classmate and friend, for a long time. I have never known him to be possessed of such strength and power. I even deem myself superior in vigour and bodily endurance. His hand trembled as he wrote, and he often expressed his inability to write as fully and as frequently as he wished. He was greatly handicapped in this respect, and he continued to suffer from its effects until his journey to Mázindarán. The moment he unsheathed his sword, however, to repulse that savage attack, a mysterious power seemed to have suddenly transformed him. In all subsequent encounters, he was seen to be the first to spring forward and spur on his charger into the camp of the aggressor. Unaided, he would face and fight the combined forces of his opponents and would himself achieve the victory. We, who followed him in the rear, had to content ourselves with those who had already been disabled and were weakened by the blows they had sustained. His name alone was sufficient to strike terror into the hearts of his adversaries.

They fled at the mention of him; they trembled at his approach. Even those who were his constant companions were mute with wonder before him. We were stunned by the display of his stupendous force, his indomitable will and complete intrepidity. We were all convinced that he had ceased to be the Mullá Husayn whom we had known, and that in him resided a spirit which God alone could bestow."

R. Mehrabkhani, Mullá Husayn: Disciple at Dawn, pp. 194-195

The philosophy of Bahá'u'lláh deserves the best thought we can give it. I am returning the book so that other blind people who have more leisure than myself may be 'shown a ray of Divinity' and their hearts be 'bathed in an inundation of eternal love.'

I take this opportunity to thank you for your kind thought of me, and for the inspiration which even the most cursory reading of Bahá'u'lláh's life cannot fail to impart. What nobler theme than the 'good of the world and the happiness of the nations' can occupy our lives? The message of universal peace will surely prevail. It is useless to combine or conspire against an idea which has in it potency to create a new earth and a new heaven and to quicken human beings with a holy passion of service.

Helen Keller wrote this personal letter to an American Bahá'í after having read something from the Braille edition of Bahá'u'lláh and the New Era, The Bahá'í World: 1938-40

Using An Interpreter

The House of Justice has instructed us to say that in cases where a member of an Assembly is unable to communicate with other members of that Assembly where a different language is employed, there is no objection to having an interpreter present at their meetings. However, the Local Assembly itself should approve the selection of the interpreter.

On behalf of the Universal House of Justice, 13 February 1984

The same guidance applies when the Assembly wishes to meet with someone who does not speak English well enough to be understood by the Assembly, or who would need an interpreter to understand the Assembly, including persons with significant hearing impairments. Interpreters should be reminded before the meeting begins that the communications they will hear are strictly confidential and should not be divulged to anyone. Interpreting is a complex skill, requiring a high level of fluency in at least two languages, as well as significant training in the role, protocols, ethics and techniques of interpreting. Should the Assembly find it necessary to hire an interpreter, it would be a legitimate Assembly expense.

Guidelines for Local Spiritual Assemblies, issued by the National Spiritual Assembly of the Bahá'ís of United States, chapter 4

LIFE AFTER DEATH

Know thou that the soul of man is exalted above, and is independent of all infirmities of body or mind. That a sick person showeth signs of weakness is due to the hindrances that interpose themselves between his soul and his body, for the soul itself remaineth unaffected by any bodily ailments. Consider the light of the lamp. Though an external object may interfere with its radiance, the light itself continueth to shine with undiminished power. In like manner, every malady afflicting the body of man is an impediment that preventeth the soul from manifesting its inherent might and power. When it leaveth the body, however, it will evince such ascendancy, and reveal such influence as no force on earth can equal. Every pure, every refined and sanctified soul will be endowed with tremendous power, and shall rejoice with exceeding gladness.

Bahá'u'lláh, Gleanings from the Writings of Bahá'u'lláh

Therefore, it is evident that this spirit is different from the body, and that the bird is different from the cage, and that the power and penetration of the spirit is stronger without the intermediary of the body. Now, if the instrument is abandoned, the possessor of the instrument continues to act. For example, if the pen is abandoned or broken, the writer remains living and present; if a house is ruined, the owner is alive and existing. This is one of the logical evidences for the immortality of the soul.

'Abdu'l-Bahá, Some Answered Questions

Consider how a being, in the world of the womb, was deaf of ear and blind of eye, and mute of tongue; how he was bereft of any perceptions at all. But once, out of that world of darkness, he passed into this world of light, then his eye saw, his ear heard, his tongue spoke. In the same way, once he hath hastened away from this mortal place into the Kingdom of God, then he will be born in the spirit; then the eye of his perception will open, the ear of his soul will hearken, and all the truths of which he was ignorant before will be made plain and clear.

'Abdu'l-Bahá, Selections from the Writings of 'Abdu'l-Bahá

As to those souls who are born into this life as ethereal and radiant entities and yet, on account of their handicaps and trials, are deprived of great and real advantages, and leave the world without having lived to the full - certainly this is a cause for grieving. This is the reason why the universal Manifestations of God unveil Their countenances to man, and endure every calamity and sore affliction, and lay down Their lives as a ransom; it is to make these very people, the ready ones, the ones who have capacity, to become dawning points of light, and to bestow upon them the life that fadeth never. This is the true sacrifice: the offering of oneself, even as did Christ, as a ransom for the life of the world.

'Abdu'l-Bahá, Selections from the Writings of 'Abdu'l-Bahá

In the next world, man will find himself freed from many of the disabilities under which he now suffers. Those who have passed on through death have a sphere of their own. It is not removed from ours; their work, the work of the kingdom, is ours; but it is sanctified from what we call 'time and place'. Time with us is measured by the sun. When there is no more sunrise, and no more sunset, that kind of time does not exist for man. Those who have ascended have different attributes from those who are still on earth, yet there is no real separation.

In prayer there is a mingling of station, a mingling of condition. Pray for them as they pray for you!

'Abdu'l-Bahá, 'Abdu'l-Bahá in London, pp. 95-96

The Bahá'í Faith

The Bahá'í Faith is an independent world religion, established in all countries and territories throughout the world. Bahá'ís come from over 2,100 ethnic, racial, and tribal groups and number some 8 million worldwide.

For more than a century, Bahá'í communities around the globe have been working to break down barriers of prejudice between peoples and have collaborated with other like-minded groups to promote the model of a global society. At the heart of Bahá'í belief is the conviction that humanity is a single people with a common destiny. In the words of Bahá'u'lláh, the Founder of the Faith, "The earth is but one country, and mankind its citizens."

Bahá'u'lláh taught that there is one God Who progressively reveals His will to humanity. Each of the great religions brought by the Messengers of God—Moses, Krishna, Buddha, Zoroaster, Jesus, Muhammad—represents a successive stage in the spiritual development of civilization. Bahá'u'lláh, the most recent Messenger in this line, has brought teachings that address the moral and spiritual challenges of the modern world.

BIOGRAPHICAL NOTES[1]

Bahá'u'lláh (1817-1892) Founder of the Bahá'í Faith, Who proclaimed that the human race is on the verge of attaining its long awaited maturity, a condition prophesied of old as the Kingdom of God on earth. Bahá'u'lláh's challenging claim is that He is the Messenger of God to this new age, sent to guide humanity through the troubled times it now faces. Imprisoned and persecuted for His teachings by the religious and civil authorities of His day, Bahá'u'lláh endured 40 years of exile from His native Persia, and finally passed away at Bahjí, just outside 'Akká, in the Holy Land.

The Báb (1819-1850) Prophet and Herald of the coming of Bahá'u'lláh. His Writings, along with those of Bahá'u'lláh, are considered by Bahá'ís to be the revealed Word of God. The Báb's teachings of the advent of a new Revelation were received with violent opposition from the rulers of Persia, who eventually had Him publicly executed. His Shrine, on the slopes of Mount Carmel in the Holy Land, has become famed for its beauty, and is known as the 'Queen of Carmel'.

'Abdu'l-Bahá (1844-1921) Eldest son of Bahá'u'lláh, appointed by Him 'Centre of the Covenant'. Having endured imprisonment and exile with His Father from an early age, 'Abdu'l-Bahá was freed in 1908. Shortly thereafter He set out to spread news of Bahá'u'lláh's

---

1 Extracts from *Behold Me: Bahá'í Writings on Unity*, p. 131

teachings in Egypt, Europe and North America, where He was widely acclaimed as the 'Prophet of Peace'.

Shoghi Effendi (1897-1957) Grandson of 'Abdu'l-Bahá, appointed by Him Guardian and World Head of the Bahá'í Faith in His Will and Testament. From 1921 until his own passing, Shoghi Effendi dedicated himself to firmly establishing the Bahá'í administrative order, to providing authoritative translations of the Bahá'í sacred Writings, and to moulding the diverse followers of Bahá'u'lláh into a single, world-wide community, conscious of its own identity and unity.

The Universal House of Justice (first elected in 1963) Ordained by Bahá'u'lláh in His Most Holy Book, this institution now stands as the central authority of the Bahá'í Faith. Its nine members are elected at an international convention every five years by members of all Bahá'í National Spiritual Assemblies throughout the world.

Guidelines for Improving Accessibility

As our communities become more accessible and inclusive, we're learning to understand that the spiritual principle of diversity can release a significant energy and facilitate advancement in our communities when everyone is included. It is important to recognize that accessibility is everyone's responsibility, and everyone benefits from it. The general principle is to preserve dignity and autonomy for persons with disabilities.

The process of providing accessibility requires removing physical barriers, changing attitudes and providing relevant support, communication or technology to ensure that all persons with disabilities are part of community life. Therefore, the goal of this section is to provide practical information to guide and assist individuals and communities in their efforts to make events such as conferences, workshops, Feasts,[1] Local Spiritual Assembly meetings,[2] and other public functions more accessible to everyone. Since each person has diverse

---

1   The Nineteen Day Feast is held on the first day of every Bahá'í month, and brings together the members of the Bahá'í community for worship, consultation and fellowship.
2   Elected annually, Local Spiritual Assemblies consist of nine Bahá'ís, and govern the affairs of each local Bahá'í community.

needs, it would be best to ask directly what specific accommodations they need, and then work on a plan of action to remove the barriers. This requires consultation, sensitivity, creativity, and an openness to work out the practical solutions.

Planning Public Events

- Planning for accessibility from the beginning improves the chances for creating an event that is enjoyable for all participants.
- The hybrid model has become standard practice in the community and there is the responsibility to make sure accommodations and technology are considered.
- An effective strategy for managing accessibility efforts is to establish an advisory committee representing a range of disabilities to oversee all phases of the event, from planning to completion. This is especially important for larger events. For smaller events, invite and encourage persons with disabilities to guide and assist with the planning process of the event.
- Local and national disability groups, organizations, and social agencies are excellent resources for information and advice and can help you find a variety of services.
- Site selection may have the greatest overall impact on accessibility to an event. Check the venue for inaccessible architectural features when selecting a home, restaurant, meeting room, or other facility so wheelchair users and others with mobility limitations can participate.
- Use an accessibility checklist, which is a tool to assess the level of accessibility of public facilities such as conference centres, etc., prior to the event being held, preferably before the facility is booked.

- The registration forms should include a section to identify whether a person has special needs and what accommodations are required to participate.
- At larger events, designate someone to be responsible for accommodations as well as help with seating, ensuring captioning and other technology is working, maintaining clear pathways, and other needs.
- Maps, floor plans, pamphlets, schedules, directional signs, information sheets, etc., should be available and displayed so persons with disabilities are aware of what is accessible to them.
- For large or medium-sized gatherings, reserve the front row seats for persons with disabilities.
- Allow those with special needs to enter into the meeting rooms before others.
- Some persons with disabilities or health conditions (visual, hearing, mobility, or medical) use service dogs. Provide comfortable space for service dogs to rest during event, and do not pet the service dogs.
- Inform the public when accommodations for persons with disabilities will be available ahead of time to make them feel included. Use International Symbols of Accessibility to promote and publicize the accessibility features of the events.
- Speak directly to the person with the disability, not to a third party. Talking with persons with disabilities is like talking with any other person.
- If you offer assistance, wait until the offer is accepted, then listen or ask for instructions.

Accessibility for Deaf & Hard of Hearing

- First find out the person who is deaf or hard of hearing's means of communication; speech, listening, lipreading, and/or sign language.
- Face the person directly and make eye contact.
- Speak clearly and distinctly, and do not exaggerate mouth movements. Use normal speed unless asked to slow down.
- Keep your face clear of obstacles which includes your hand, a microphone or any other object.
- If the person has difficulty understanding a particular phrase or word, try a different way of saying the same thing by rephrasing the sentence.
- Reduce background noise because many people with hearing loss have greater difficulty understanding speech. Avoid situations where there will be loud sounds when possible.
- Make sure the physical arrangements make communication more accessible such as sufficient lighting and sitting in a circle. Make sure the person who is hard of hearing has their back to the light, including the windows.
- In a group setting, repeat questions or key facts to make sure everyone understood what was being said.
- Provide pertinent information in writing, such as directions, names, phone numbers, etc.
- Use technology by typing back and forth on a computer screen, using email, instant messenger or text messaging.

- Enable captions / live transcript for Zoom meetings. (click on settings, click on 'In Meeting' (Basic), turn on 'Closed Captions' to ON). It's free and automatic.
- Turn on CC (Closed Captions) on videos, and TV screens for both online and in- person events.
- Use Otter (Otter.ai) and other programs which transcribe speech to text. This is useful for recording meetings and taking notes for both virtual and in-person meetings.
- Use a good quality microphone at workshops and meetings to assist individuals to hear better.
- Rent or provide Assistive Listening Devices such as an FM system, Infrared system, loop (audio induction), and Bluetooth systems. All can be used with or without hearing aids or a cochlear implant. Contact the agencies that serve persons who are deaf and hard of hearing for these systems.
- There are a variety of ways to use the phone – Telecommunications relay service, IP relay service, video relay service, hearing aid compatible phones, videophones, captioned or amplified phones, TTY, etc.
- Arrange for Sign Language Interpreters for individuals who use American Sign Language (ASL).
- If the person uses sign language and you know any sign language, try using it and your attempts will be appreciated.
- When planning meetings for a Feast or Assembly meeting, provide visual aids and printed materials such as letters, prayers, and Holy Writings or send them online.

- Emergency alerting devices such as fire alarms should be visual (i.e. flashing lights) as well as audio.
- Inform the public when captions / live transcript and other accommodations will be available ahead of time to make everyone feel included.

Accessibility for Blind & Low Vision

- First find out what mediums a person can use; large print, screen readers, digital audio files, or Braille. Never assume that a person who is visual impaired knows Braille; many are unable to read it.
- When beginning an activity, make sure to introduce someone who is visual impaired to their surroundings. Many people who are visually impaired feel comfortable travelling independently, however there may be times when a guide may be needed. Ask them how they would like to be guided.
- Introduce yourself by name and wait for them to offer their hand to be shaken. Unexpected touches can startle or be uncomfortable for the individual.
- Speak in a normal tone, speed, and volume. Address them directly, and not to the person they are with.
- To guide a person who is blind, first ask them if they want assistance, and then let them take your arm. The individual will walk about half a step behind you, following your body motions. If you encounter steps, curbs, doors, or other obstacles, identify them in spoken language.
- When giving directions, be as clear and specific as possible and check for understanding. Make sure the person knows when you have finished and are moving away from them.
- There are a range of screen readers which transmits whatever text is displayed on the computer screen into a form that a person with vision loss can process

(speech, Braille or a combination of both). Some examples are JAWS, VoiceOver, TalkBack, Siri, Kurzweil, Alexa, Google Maps, Google Home, etc.

- Use iPhones and other tools to read menus and more complex documents. Make word documents accessible using headings, and PDF documents into searchable PDF docs as opposed to image-only.
- Printed materials, prayers and Holy Writings could be provided using the person's format of choice.
- If there are persons who are blind or have vision loss in your community; you will need to make sure that they have transportation to Feasts, public meetings, etc. Providing rides is much better since it's more convenient and supportive.
- There are transportation services such as buses, cabs, light rail transit, and mobility transport. If using these services, it may require time and money to arrange. The biggest challenge for persons who are visually impaired is to navigate around places, which requires extra planning to get around safely and independently.
- Check to see if elevators have either Braille, engraved numbers, bell signals or speech.

Accessibility for Mobility Difficulties

- Work with hosts in private homes for events to arrange what assistance they might need such as getting into the home.
- A person's mobility equipment, such as a wheelchair, scooter or cane, is part of their personal space. Therefore, do not lean against or touch the equipment.
- Do not assume a wheelchair user or person who uses a walker wants help. If you see a situation where the person could use your assistance, ask first.
- When embarking down a path with multiple obstacles, ask "What's the easiest way for you to do this?" Listen and follow their instructions carefully.
- Individuals who have difficulty with mobility may be stopped by barriers most people don't notice such as a high curb or a flight of stairs.
- Check that there are accessible parking spaces close to the entrance of the venue reserved for persons with mobility difficulties. Indicate where the parking is located in the registration material.
- Some individuals find ramps much safer and easier to use than stairs. Ensure that the main entrances have accessible ramps in identifiable locations and with a proper incline (i.e. not too steep of an incline). A ramp can be permanent or portable.
- Curb cuts into sidewalks (footpath) make it easier for wheelchair and walker users to get onto or off the sidewalks easily.

- Doorways need to be wide enough for a wheelchair user to enter. The doors should not be heavy and difficult to open. Look for automatic door openers.
- It's easier if hallways have good smooth floor covering such as wood, linoleum or non-slip tiles since carpets can be difficult for wheelchair and walker users.
- Check for elevators in the building if there is more than one floor. The elevator controls need to be within the reach of a wheelchair user.
- Rest-rooms should be equipped with grab bars in key locations to increase safety and more support.
- The doorways to the rest-room need to be a minimum 32 inches (~81 cm) wide. In tight spaces, the door should open outwards from the rest-room. Door lever handles need to be on both the inside and outside of the door.
- The sinks need to be low enough with space for wheelchair users to place their legs underneath and the pipes (hot water) are far enough back so that the person will not burn their legs. Use faucets with level handles which are easy to turn on and off.
- The toilet paper dispensers, towel machines, hand driers, soap, coat hooks and other dispensers need to be within reach of wheelchair users.
- Remove obstacles (i.e. ornamental plants) and arrange furniture to ensure clear passage so the person with mobility difficulties can move around easily.

BIBLIOGRAPHY

'Abdu'l-Bahá, *'Abdu'l-Bahá in London: Addresses and Notes of Conversations*. London: Bahá'í Publishing Trust, 1912, 1st ed., reprinted 1987.

'Abdu'l-Bahá, *Foundations of World Unity*. Wilmette: Bahá'í Publishing Trust, 1979.

'Abdu'l-Bahá, *Paris Talks: Addresses given by 'Abdu'l-Bahá in Paris in 1911-1912*. Bahá'í Reference Library: www.bahai.org/library/authoritative-texts/abdul-baha/paris-talks/

'Abdu'l-Bahá, *The Promulgation of Universal Peace: Discourses by 'Abdu'l-Bahá During His Visit to the United States in 1912*. Bahá'í Reference Library: www.bahai.org/library/authoritative-texts/abdul-baha/promulgation-universal-peace/

'Abdu'l-Bahá, *Selections from the Writings of 'Abdu'l-Bahá*. Bahá'í Reference Library: www.bahai.org/library/authoritative-texts/abdul-baha/selections-writings-abdul-baha/

'Abdu'l-Bahá, *Some Answered Questions*. Bahá'í Reference Library: www.bahai.org/library/authoritative-texts/abdul-baha/some-answered-questions/

'Abdu'l-Bahá, *The Secret of Divine Civilization*. Bahá'í Reference Library: www.bahai.org/library/authoritative-texts/abdul-baha/secret-divine-civilization/

'Abdu'l-Bahá, *Tablets of 'Abdu'l-Bahá Abbas*. New York: Bahá'í Publishing Committee; vol. 1, 1930; vol. 2, 1940; vol. 3, 1930.

The Báb, *Selections from the Writings of the Báb*. Bahá'í Reference Library: www.bahai.org/library/authoritative-texts/the-bab/selections-writings-bab/

The Bahá'í Life: Excerpts from the Writings of the Guardian. Compiled by the Universal House of Justice. Canada: National Spiritual Assembly of the Bahá'ís of Canada, 1973.

Bahá'í Marriage and Family Life (compilation). Compiled by the National Spiritual Assembly of the Bahá'ís of Canada, 1983.

Bahá'í News. National Spiritual Assembly of the Bahá'ís of United States, January 1952.

Bahá'í Prayers: Prayers of Bahá'u'lláh, the Báb, and 'Abdu'l-Bahá. Bahá'í Reference Library: www.bahai.org/library/authoritative-texts/prayers/

Bahá'í Readings: Selections from the Writings of The Báb, Bahá'u'lláh and 'Abdu'l-Bahá for daily meditation. Canada: National Spiritual Assembly of the Bahá'ís of Canada, 1984.

The Bahá'í World: 1925–1926. New York: Bahá'í Publishing Committee, 1926.

The Bahá'í World: 1932–34. New York: Bahá'í Publishing Committee, 1936.

The Bahá'í World: 1938–40. Wilmette: Bahá'í Publishing Trust, 1942.

Bahá'í World Faith: Selected Writings of Bahá'u'lláh and 'Abdu'l-Bahá. Wilmette: Bahá'í Publishing Trust, 4th printing, 1969.

Bahá'u'lláh, *Epistle to the Son of the Wolf.* Bahá'í Reference Library: www.bahai.org/library/authoritative-texts/bahaullah/epistle-son-wolf/

Bahá'u'lláh, *Gleanings from the Writings of Bahá'u'lláh.* Bahá'í Reference Library: www.bahai.org/library/authoritative-texts/ bahaullah/gleanings-writings-bahaullah/

Bahá'u'lláh, *The Kitáb-i-Aqdas: The Most Holy Book.* Bahá'í Reference Library: www.bahai.org/library/authoritative-texts/bahaullah/ kitab-i-aqdas/

Bahá'u'lláh, *Tablets of Bahá'u'lláh revealed after the Kitáb-i-Aqdas.* Bahá'í Reference Library: www.bahai.org/library/ authoritative-texts/bahaullah/tablets-bahaullah/

Bahá'u'lláh, *Writings of Bahá'u'lláh* (compilation). India: Bahá'í Publishing Trust, 1986.

Balyuzi, H. M., *'Abdu'l-Bahá: The Centre of the Covenant of Bahá'u'lláh.* Oxford: George Ronald, 1971.

Behold Me: Bahá'í Writings on Unity. Based on a compilation originally prepared by George Allen. London: Bahá'í Publishing Trust, 1995.

Blomfield, Lady (Sitárih Khánum), *The Chosen Highway.* London: Bahá'í Publishing Trust, 1940; Wilmette: Bahá'í Publishing Trust, 1970.

Brown, R. A., *Memories of 'Abdu'l-Bahá: Recollections of the Early Days of the Bahá'í Faith in California.* Wilmette: Bahá'í PublishingTrust, 1980.

Consultation (compilation). Bahá'í Reference Library: www.bahai.org/library/authoritative-texts/compilations/consultation/

Esslemont, J. E., *Bahá'u'lláh and the New Era.* George Allen & Unwin Ltd., 1923, Wilmette: Bahá'í Publishing Trust, 1980, 5th. ed.

Freeman, D., *From Copper to Gold: The Life of Dorothy Baker.* Oxford: George Ronald, 1984.

Green Acre on the Piscataqua. Compiled by The Green Acre Bahá'í School Council. Maine: National Spiritual Assembly of the Bahá'ís of the United States, 1991.

Health and Healing (compilation). Compiled by the Research Department of the Universal House of Justice. New Delhi: Bahá'í Publishing Trust, 1994, 3rd ed.

Honnold, A., *Vignettes from the Life of 'Abdu'l-Bahá*. George Ronald, Oxford, 1982, reprinted 1997.

Individual Rights and Freedoms in the World Order of Bahá'u'lláh - A Statement by The Universal House of Justice. Wilmette, Bahá'í Publishing Trust, 1989.

Ives, H. C., *Portals to Freedom*. Oxford: George Ronald, 1937, reprinted 1983.

Lights of Guidance, A Bahá'í Reference File. Compiled by Helen Hornby. India: Bahá'í Publishing Trust, 1988, 2nd ed.

Living the Life (compilation). Issued by the Universal House of Justice, November, 1972. London: Bahá'í Publishing Trust, 1974, reprinted 1984.

McLean, J., *A Love That Could Not Wait*. Essex, Maryland: One Voice Press, 2016

Maxwell, M., *An Early Pilgrimage*. London: George Ronald, 1917, reprinted 1970.

Mehrabkhani, R., *Mullá Husayn: Disciple at Dawn*. Los Angeles: Kalimát Press, 1987.

The Pattern of Bahá'í Life (compilation). London: Bahá'í Publishing Trust, 1948, reprinted 1983.

Perkins, M., *Hour of the Dawn: The Life of the Báb*. Oxford: George Ronald, 1987.

The Power of Divine Assistance (compilation). Compiled by the Research Department of the Universal House of Justice. Canada: National Spiritual Assembly of the Bahá'ís of Canada, 1982.

Principles of Bahá'í Administration (compilation). London: Bahá'í Publishing Trust, 1973, 3rd ed.

Quickeners of Mankind - Pioneering in a World Community. The National Spiritual Assembly of the Bahá'ís of Canada, 1980.

Rabbaní, R., *The Priceless Pearl.* London: Bahá'í Publishing Trust, 1969.

Ruhe, D., *Robe of Light: The Persian Years of the Supreme Prophet Bahá'u'lláh, 1817-1853.* Oxford: George Ronald, 1994.

Shoghi Effendi, *The Advent of Divine Justice.* Bahá'í Reference Library: www.bahai.org/library/authoritative-texts/shoghi-effendi/advent-divine-justice/

Shoghi Effendi, *Citadel of Faith: Messages to America, 1947-1957.* Bahá'í Reference Library: www.bahai.org/library/authoritative-texts/shoghi-effendi/citadel-faith/

Shoghi Effendi, *Dawn of a New Day: Messages to India, 1923-1957.* New Delhi: Bahá'í Publishing Trust, 1970.

Shoghi Effendi, God Passes By. Bahá'í Reference Library: www.bahai.org/library/authoritative-texts/shoghi-effendi/god-passes-by/

Shoghi Effendi, *The Unfolding Destiny of the British Bahá'í Community: Messages of the Guardian of the Bahá'í Faith to the Bahá'ís of the British Isles.* London: Bahá'í Publishing Trust, 1981.

Shoghi Effendi, *High Endeavors: Messages to Alaska.* National Spiritual Assembly of the Bahá'ís of Alaska, Inc., 1976.

Shoghi Effendi, *The World Order of Bahá'u'lláh.* Bahá'í Reference Library: www.bahai.org/library/authoritative-texts/shoghi-effendi/world-order-bahaullah/

Spiritual Foundations: Prayer, Meditation and the Devotional Attitude (compilation). Compiled by the Research Department of the Universal House of Justice. Wilmette: Bahá'í Publishing Trust, 1980.

Star of the West: Volume VIII. Chicago: Bahá'í News Service, 1917.

Star of the West: The Bahá'í Magazine, Volume XIV. Committee for the National Spiritual Assembly of America, 1923.

Taherzadeh, A., *The Covenant of Bahá'u'lláh*. Oxford: George Ronald, 1992.

Taherzadeh, A., *The Revelation of Bahá'u'lláh*. Vols. 1 and 2. Oxford: George Ronald, 1988.

Taherzadeh, A., *Trustees of the Merciful*. London: Bahá'í Publishing Trust, 1972.

The Universal House of Justice, letter to the National Spiritual Assembly of the Bahá'ís of the United States, 11 September 1995.

Ward, A. L., *239 Days: 'Abdu'l-Bahá's Journey in America*. Wilmette: Bahá'í Publishing Trust, 1979.

Weil, H. A., *Closer Than Your Life-Vein*. United States: National Spiritual Assembly of the Bahá'ís of Alaska, 1978.

Weinberg, R., *Ethel Jenner Rosenberg: The Life and Times of England's Outstanding Bahá'í Pioneer Worker*. Oxford: George Ronald, 1995.

www.ingramcontent.com/pod-product-compliance
Lightning Source LLC
Chambersburg PA
CBHW050529280326
41933CB00011B/1522